Sven Lindqvist was the author of more than thirty books, including *"Exterminate All the Brutes," A History of Bombing, Terra Nullius,* and *The Dead Do Not Die* (all published by The New Press). A resident of Stockholm, he held a PhD in the history of literature from Stockholm University, an honorary doctorate from Uppsala University, and an honorary professorship from the Swedish government.

Also by Sven Lindqvist

"Exterminate All the Brutes":
One Man's Odyssey into the Heart of Darkness and the Origins of European Genocide

The Skull Measurer's Mistake

And Other Portraits of Men and Women Who Spoke Out Against Racism

Sven Lindqvist

Translated from the Swedish by Joan Tate

The New Press
New York

First published by Albert Bonniers Forlag AB, Stockholm
Published in the United States by The New Press, New York, 1997
Distributed by Two Rivers Distribution

ISBN 978-1-56584-363-9 (hc)
ISBN 978-1-62097-710-1 (pb)
ISBN 978-1-62097-709-5 (ebook)
CIP data is available

The New Press publishes books that promote and enrich public discussion and understanding of the issues vital to our democracy and to a more equitable world. These books are made possible by the enthusiasm of our readers; the support of a committed group of donors, large and small; the collaboration of our many partners in the independent media and the not-for-profit sector; booksellers, who often hand-sell New Press books; librarians; and above all by our authors.

www.thenewpress.com

Printed in the United States of America

10 9 8 7 6 5 4 3 2 1

To Clara, for whom this book was written.

Contents

The Skull Measurer's Mistake

Preface

THE HISTORY OF racism is not only about racists. Throughout history there have also been people who have seen through the errors of racists and protested against their abuses. This book is about some of those people.

My selection is of necessity subjective. I have not striven for completeness, and I make no claim to have made any scholarly discovery. I have simply read works by eighteenth- and nineteenth-century antiracists and their opponents, as well as some important works in scholarly literature on racism and antiracism and attempted to chronicle some of those struggles.

The antiracists I present here are not free of the prejudices of their times; they share some, while combating others. The fact that they are all Europeans or North Americans is not because antiracism does not exist in, for instance, the Far East or the Arab world, but is a result of my own ignorance.

My aim—it goes without saying—is not to give an overall view of Europe and its relations with its minorities and the rest of the world. My aim is quite simply to remind readers of some antiracists, who today are often forgotten, and as far as I know have never been discussed together. I also hope to show those who are today fighting against racism something of the long and proud tradition to which they belong.

Sven Lindqvist

Introduction

The Western world wishes to forget its racist past, says Stephen Wilson in his great study of French anti-Semitism. *Ideology and Experience* (1982). As a result of this forgetfulness a vast chapter in the thought of the West has been conjured away. He quotes another historian of racism, Leon Poliakov, "this vanishing trick represents a collective repression of troubling memories and awkward truths."

I have tried to avoid this. I describe racism as one of the dominating ideologies of the nineteenth century—with emphasis on a few men and women who had the courage to go against the mainstream and criticize the racial prejudices of their day.

Racist ideology, as I see it, has its source in a need to legitimize violence and oppression.

Europeans needed to justify their conquest of North America, South America, Southern Africa, Siberia, Australia, and the Pacific Islands. Most of all, they had to absolve themselves of guilt for the almost total extermination of the previous inhabitants of these huge areas. At first, religious explanations dominated, but during the nineteenth century the belief arose that it was the Europeans' destiny to conquer and exterminate and that the other races were destined to be conquered and exterminated.

Those who fought against this racism of conquest include Benjamin Franklin, William Howitt, Langfield Ward, Helen Hunt, and Olive Schreiner.

White society's need to legitimize the enslavement of Africans and later to defend the continued oppression of ex-slaves and their descendants is another source of racism. In this case, too, religious arguments were replaced during the nineteenth century by biological ones. It was maintained that whites were born to rule and blacks to subjection. To attempt to change this went against nature, according to prevailing ideology—not only in the former slave states, but also in British, French, Belgian, Dutch, and German colonies; in fact almost everywhere where whites came across blacks.

Those who fought against slavery and oppression of black people include: Granville Sharp, James Ramsay, Friedrich Tiedemann, George Cable, and Mary Kingsley.

Racist ideology has also been used to dispose of troublesome competitors and aliens who appear frightening. Racists declare certain groups of immigrants biologically inferior and incapable of integrating with existing society. That was said of the Chinese and Japanese in the nineteenth-century in the United States, and is said today of Chicanos in the United States, and of "Arabs" in France. Immigrants themselves are not immune to hatred of other immigrants—in the United States, the despised Irish immigrants were particularly hostile to, for instance, Chinese and Jewish immigration.

Those who spoke against hatred of immigrants and for free competition between different races include Raphael Pumpelly and Jacques Novicow.

In Europe, anti-Semitism has been the most common and the most virulent form of racism. There, too, the motivation was originally religious; but during the latter half of the nineteenth century, hatred of Jews returned in a new biological disguise that was used to defend discrimination, exclusion from professions, special laws, and finally the murder by Hitler of six million Jews during World War II.

Theodor Mommsen and Anatole Leroy-Beaulieu were among the few who saw early on where anti-Semitism was heading and tried to prevent its spread.

There are no sharp boundaries between these four forms of racism. When the Jews were allowed to leave the ghetto, they became in a sense "immigrants" in countries in which they had lived for centuries. When black slaves in the Unites States were allowed to leave the plantations, they became "immigrants" in free society, often moving from former slave states to the industrial North. It could be said that the surviving indigenous peoples in America, Australia, etc., once their lands had been taken, became "immigrants" in the slums of the white societies that had replaced their own. The differences between these groups are obvious, but there is also something similar in their displacement by a dominating majority.

Sometimes antiracists have seen this common thread and spoken for more than one race—Henri Grégoire for both Jews and blacks, Alexis de Tocqueville for both blacks and Native Americans; more often though, anti racists fought for a single group.

This applies to the scholars as well. Those who study the

fate of Native Americans have seldom paid attention to the situation of the blacks, the Chinese, or the Jews—and vice versa. This is a pity, for it seems obvious to me that there are racist ideas and "solutions" that have shifted between various forms of racism and been applied to one object of hate after another. One example of this is the way the image of "the dying Indian" led to wishful dreams that the "Negro," the "Semite," the "Mongol," even all the "inferior races" were dying out.

Native Americans and blacks in the nineteenth century had as yet very few highly educated intellectuals who could speak for them and criticize the theories declaring them to be born inferior. Among the Jews, on the other hand, there were many highly qualified intellectuals, who now had good reason to examine racial theories, because they were being directed at the Jewish people. When criticism of the basic assumptions of racism was again taken up at the turn of the century in 1900, several of the critics were of Jewish origin.

Something similar applied to the Irish. That a people who had produced William Butler Yeats and George Bernard Shaw should be so biologically deficient that they could not rule themselves, but would have to remain for ever under British supremacy—that was a paradox hard to digest, not least for the Irish themselves. They were among the very first to criticize the fundaments of racism at the end of the nineteenth century.

Several early antiracists were also feminists. The women's movement questioned the myth that woman was biologically inferior to man, and some in the movement went on to doubt the racists' related statement that blacks were biologically inferior to whites.

This book ends in 1899. During the late nineteenth century, the numbers of antiracists increased to include such people as William Babington, John Mackinnon Robertson, Jacques Novicow, Joseph Conrad, Anatole Leroy-Beaulieu, Mary Kingsley, Olive Schreiner, and Theophilus Scholes. They also spoke with greater authority than had the antiracists of before. A turning point was approaching. But it had still not yet arrived.

It was not until 1911 that a leading social scientist, Franz Boas, repudiated the scientific basis of racism. Three more decades were to pass before his standpoint ceased to be controversial. Meanwhile, the practice of racism became increasingly horrific, particularly in Hitler's Germany and, until his death, Stalin's Soviet Union. Not until racism culminated in the the murder of six million Jews during World War II were the world's leading biologists and social scientists able to agree in a UNESCO declaration of 1950 that racist ideology was a false doctrine lacking any scientific evidence.

Naturally, this did not mean that racism was overcome. The fight against racism continues and is today more necessary than ever. The antiracists of today need a history. Fractions of such a history are contained in this book.

1

The Discovery of Prejudices

Benjamin Franklin, 1764

On Wednesday, December 14, 1763, the Paxton boys came riding through the night and encircled the Indian village of Conestogoe in Lancaster, Pennsylvania. They were fifty or so armed men, and at dawn they attacked the village and killed every Indian they found: three old men, two women, and a boy.

When the young Indians returned, they found among the ruins the half-burned bodies of their murdered parents and relatives.

It had happened again. The indiscriminate slaughter of North American Indians was to continue for the rest of the eighteenth century. It was to go on all through the nineteenth century and not end until after the massacre at Wounded Knee in 1890, by which time the Native American population had been almost totally decimated.

Not everyone was on the side of the murderers. In Lancaster, the authorities tried to rescue the remaining fourteen Indians by putting them in a workhouse. That was the only place where their safety was considered guaranteed.

But on December 27, the Paxton boys came back to Lancaster with a large crowd of supporters and broke down the workhouse door. The Indians had neither weapons with which to defend themselves nor any means of escaping. They fell to their knees and begged for their lives. In that position, they were struck down with axes. None survived.

Cheering as if they had won a great victory, the murderers rode away. No one stopped them. No one wanted to or dared to claim the reward—200 pounds—which the authorities were offering for information that might lead to their capture.

The Paxton boys had now tasted blood. In February 1764, with several hundred men, they marched toward Philadelphia. The governor had no police force to halt such numbers, and he was responsible for 140 Indians who had sought shelter in the town.

In his need, he called on Benjamin Franklin. At the time, Franklin was neither the world-famous inventor of the lightning conductor nor the esteemed diplomat and statesman. Franklin was a fifty-year-old printer of books, primarily known for having organized the home guard in Pennsylvania and having led the colony's defense during the war against the Indians and the French.

Franklin had no reputation of being "soft on Indians." If anyone could put the white mob to rights, then it was he.

Franklin undertook the assignment. He rode alone to meet the murderers, confronting them in Germantown, seven miles outside Philadelphia.

What did he say?

What would I have said?

In the 1870s, a new word—"prejudice"—had just begun to appear in the American English. From the beginning, it signified just a "prejudgment," a judgment made before the hearing and the trial had even begun.

The word came from France, where Diderot's *Encyclopédie* defined it "PREJUDICE—false judgment on the nature of things, caused by insufficient use of intellectual faculties; the unfortunate product of an ignorance that blinds and imprisons the mind."

Frenchmen of the Enlightenment were criticizing the religious prejudices of the priesthood against dissidents and the class prejudices of the aristocracy. In America, where there was neither a nobility nor a state church, the concept was applied primarily to relations between the races.

Samuel Hopkins was one of the first to realize that "our education has filled us with strong prejudices," and led us to consider blacks, "not as our brethren, or in any degrees on a level with us; but as quite another species of animals, made only to serve us and our children . . ." And the Quaker, John Woolman, wrote in his essays, published from Franklin's printing works, that if right from childhood we have always seen black people badly dressed, always compliant, and forced to do dirty work, "then it tends gradually to fix a Notion in the Mind, that they are the Sort of People below us in Nature."

And if from early childhood one has heard nothing about the Indians except how cruel, unreliable, and depraved they are, then that is the image carried in the mind. What makes a man raise his axe is not the real Indian in front of him, but the image in his mind of an evil and dangerous Indian who has to be eliminated.

Franklin realized this. But how could he explain that to several hundred bloodthirsty skinheads on their way to Philadelphia to kill Indians? How could he in a few hours replace the image decades of hatred had built up in their minds with a more realistic one?

It was an almost impossible assignment.

He began by appealing to a stereotype—the idea of the Indians dying out by themselves. "It has always been observed," he said, "that Indians settled in the Neighbourhood of White People, do not increase, but diminish continually." That was also true of Conestogoe, where only twenty Indians were left out of the once numerous tribe.

The implication was clear: was it not unnecessary to kill the remains of the tribe, which was anyhow dying out on its own?

Franklin also talked about those who had been murdered in Conestogoe the previous year. He named them. The eldest was called Shehaes and he was old enough to have met the founder of Pennsylvania, William Penn. He was being cared for in his old age by his daughter Peggy. She had a three-year-old son with her husband John. Toothless old Betty lived with her son Peter. There were also two brothers, George and Will, and a childless woman, Sally, who had adopted an orphan child.

So they all had names. They were not wild animals in the forest, but human beings with kinfolk they took care of and who had ordinary English names, names which said nothing about the color of their skin. Franklin made a special point of that. When the Indians give their children English names, he said, it was out of admiration for the English and a desire to emulate them.

But it was no use. All of them had been killed. When Peggy went back to the village, she found old Shehaes murdered and mutilated in his bed. Peter had found his mother's old body, scalped and hideously violated.

The murdered Indians were the last remains of a people who had once belonged to the Indian federation called Six Nations. When the English first arrived in Pennsylvania, representatives of this people went to welcome them with gifts of meat, grain, and hides. They made a treaty with William Penn, promising friendship "as long as the Sun should shine, or the Waters run in the Rivers."

That treaty had been constantly renewed and neither side had broken it—not until now, when the Paxton boys broke it.

The question is: If an Indian has done an injustice to me, does that give me the right to take revenge on all other Indians? The Indians, just like the whites, belong to different nations and speak different languages. If the French commit an injustice toward the Dutch, have the Dutch then the right to take revenge on the English? If a man's wife is murdered by a freckle-faced, red-haired man, has he because of that the right to kill all freckle-faced and red-haired women and children he comes across? The only crime these Indians had committed was having the same reddish-brown skin color as some other Indians who had committed murder. Is that sufficient reason to murder them?

It is unnecessary, Franklin said, to say more about the rumors circulating about the poor wretches who have been murdered and about the 140 Christian Indians you are now threatening to murder. If you are acquainted with these Indians, then you know that the stories are pure inventions contrived to incite to murder, or to justify already committed outrages. With this, I am publicly challenging anyone who has such accusations to step forward and prove them.

If Will Soc, murdered in the workhouse in Lancaster, had truly been guilty of what he is now accused of, why has he not been taken to court? Is it English justice to condemn and execute him unheard?

And what wrong had old Sheheas done? And the children? Babies still at the breast, how have they deserved being shot?

Killing children, said Franklin, is not only inhuman, it is cowardly and unmanly.

We call ourselves Christians, Franklin said, but these Indians would have been safer among the ancient heathens, with whom the rites of hospitality were sacred, than they are among us Christians in Pennsylvania. They would have been safer with the Turks, with the Moors, or the black savages in Africa. They would have been safer everywhere in the known world than they were here, with the white savages of Pennsylvania.

We do not know which of these arguments did it. All we know is that the march against Philadephia was halted. The Paxton boys and their followers dispersed and turned back home.

2

"Whether a Slave, by coming into England, becomes free?"

Granville Sharp, 1772

ONE EARLY MORNING in 1765, a half-blind and feverish African was staggering along Mincing Lane in London. Granville Sharp, a young clerk, spotted him and took him to his brother, a doctor.

It turned out that the African was called Jonathan Strong and had been a slave to a lawyer in Barbados, David Lisle, who had brought him with him back to England. Lisle had ill-treated his slave, hit him over the head with a pistol, then thrown him out as worn-out and useless.

The Sharp brothers ensured that Jonathan was admitted to a hospital and paid for him for four months until he had regained his sight and health. Then they found work for him with an apothecary called Brown in Fenchurch Street.

But two years later he was recognized in the street by his previous owner. When the latter saw that the slave was once again in good health and fit for work, he had him seized and sold him to a plantation in the West Indies.

While Jonathan was in custody as an escaped slave awaiting transportation to Barbados, he managed to smuggle out a letter to Granville Sharp.

The letter was almost illegible and at first Granville could not remember the name. Strong? Who was that? He sent a message to the lockup asking who Jonathan Strong was and was told there was no one there by that name.

Granville was suspicious, went to the lockup himself, and asked to speak to whoever was in charge. No, there was no Strong there. Granville persisted. Yes, of course, they did have an escaped Negro; perhaps his name was Strong.

Granville recognized Jonathan immediately. He asked to see the warrant of arrest. No, he was nothing but an escaped slave, so no warrant was required. Granville went to the chief magistrate and requested that a prisoner by the name of Jonathan Strong, at present held in custody with no warrant of arrest, should have his deprivation of liberty tested in court. That was granted.

The captain who was to transport Jonathan to Barbados appeared with papers for the sale of the slave. But the magistrate explained that as Jonathan had not committed any crime, he should be discharged.

"I take him as Mr. Lisle's property," the captain said, taking him by the arm.

"Sir, I charge you with assault," said Granville Sharp.

The captain let the man go and no one dared touch Jonathan as he left the court with Granville.

But the next day, Granville was served with a summons for having robbed Jonathan's rightful owner of his property. Granville sought help from several leading lawyers, but they all explained that he had no chance of winning the case. In whatever way a slave had been treated, he remained the property of his owner. The only way out was to hand Jonathan over immediately.

But Granville Sharp was not so easily written off. He was the son of a Durham parson and had come to London as a fifteen-year-old, first as an apprentice to a cloth merchant who was a Quaker, then a Presbyterian, and, finally, a Roman Catholic. Now he was in his thirties and had a permanent job in the civil service. He had privately learned both Greek and Hebrew and now he had also started studying law, particularly the laws concerning deprivation of liberty.

He wrote down everything he had learned in a notebook which is still preserved. In it, it is possible to follow his meandering path through the thickets of English common law and see how one day he finds Henry VIII's statute 32, which states: "Every alien and stranger are bounden by and unto the laws and statutes of this realm, and to all and singular the contents of the same."

If this applies to all foreigners, why should it not also apply to slaves? thought Granville. And if when they come to England slaves are bound by English law, then they must also enjoy the protection of the law.

"Query, whether aliens oppressed in England, under the pretence of their being slaves, may not sue their respective masters, in the King's name, for attempting forcibly to keep, detain and transport out of the kingdom as slaves, aliens that are . . . under the protection of this realm."

Granville wanted the matter tested in court. Lisle had received so much unpleasant publicity that he had long ago withdrawn the charge against Granville. So Jonathan Strong was saved. But Englishmen from the West Indies had over 15,000 blacks as slaves in England and assaults on blacks were common. It soon became known that Granville was taking up their cause—as soon as anything happened, he was called upon.

One day, a neighbor came rushing round to tell him that an African by the name of Thomas Lewis had been found by his ex-master, Stapylton, living in Chelsea. Stapylton had hired two men to lie in wait at night for the black man and they had dragged him by force on board a ship on the Thames. He was sitting there now, gagged, tied to the mast — and the ship was about to sail for Jamaica.

Granville at once went to the court and was given an injunction that the kidnapped man was to appear in court to have his case heard. The captain refused to accept the injunction as he had already had permission to sail. But just beyond the anchorage, the ship was delayed by a head wind, the summons was served, and the captain reluctantly had to hand over Thomas Lewis.

The case came up before Lord Chief Justice Mansfield. He was known as a conservative judge, closely associated with the powerful West Indian plantation interests. This time he discharged the slave by referring to the fact that Stapylton was unable to prove his right of ownership. With that, he managed to evade the main question: whether a human being, according to English law, could be the property of another at all.

But Granville Sharp continued saving slaves and finally, on February 7, 1772, Lord Chief Justice Mansfield was faced with a case in which he had to take a stand on the main question. This concerned a slave called James Somersett who had run away from his owner, Charles Stewart, but had been caught and put on board a ship to Jamaica to be sold—which owing to the hardships during transportation was often the equivalent of a death sentence.

So as not to annoy the judge, Granville Sharp kept away from the court, but he had engaged the best lawyers and supplied them with all the evidence that he had collected.

"That no man at this day is or can be a Slave in England," maintained Somersett's defense counsel. The only form of slavery that has ever existed in England is villenage and that has long ago ceased. There is no English law that allows slavery. So Somersett must be discharged, the defense maintained.

It has been stated that as Somersett is a slave according to the laws of Virginia, he should also be a slave in England. But if one of the laws of Virginia were to apply in England, then all other laws must also apply here. Or where do you wish to draw the line? And if the laws of Virginia are to apply in England, then the laws of all other countries must also apply here. Why not equally the laws of Japan or Turkey? Presuming a Turk comes here with a Christian slave, or a pasha arrives with half a dozen white women for his pleasure, is English law to apply, or Turkish?

The question is, where do you draw the line? If you declare another country's laws valid in England, then I cannot understand but that you must go all over the world to find the laws that will be valid here. May I point out that already in the days of Queen Elizabeth, a Russian brought a serf with him and went on whipping him as usual. For that he was taken to court and in the summing up it was said that "England was too pure an air for slaves to breathe in." I hope, the lawyer concluded, that the air has not become worse since then.

Judge Mansfield sighed and adjourned the proceedings until May 9. When the court convened again, the question was put in this way: "Whether a Slave, by coming into England, becomes free?"

The judge first summed up the case for Somersett. He considered the dispute as between one human creature, the Master, and another, the Negro, and whether the latter should be entitled to the important rights that nature had given him.

It was undisputed in the case that the black man had been a slave in America. The question was whether this also made him a slave in England, where no such state was admitted by law.

The lawyers speaking for Stewart never attempted to dispute that the black man was a human being or that liberty was a human right. Instead, they started out from the inviolability of property and maintained that it would be absurd and unjust to rob a man of his lawful property just because he had taken it with him from one country to another.

This was not a matter of small sums—if Somersett were discharged, slave owners in England stood to lose at least £700,000. The lawyers particularly emphasized how inexpedient and dangerous it would be to let a large number of black men loose in England.

The judge wriggled like a worm on a hook and interrupted and adjourned the proceedings over and over again. Each time the court convened, the listening public became more numerous and the waves of discussion grew.

When the judgment was finally pronounced on June 22, 1772, it turned out that Lord Chief Justice Mansfield had had a change of mind. He now accepted Granville Sharp's viewpoint. "So high an act of dominion [as slavery] must derive its force from the law of the country; and if to be justified here, must be justified by the laws of England. . . . The power claimed here never was in use here, or acknowledged by the law . . . And therefore the man must be discharged."

Granville Sharp had won the first battle in the long struggle against slavery. Black men and women could no longer be hunted like wild animals on the streets of London.

3

"Why not?"

Georg Lichtenberg, 1778

It is said that a book can't be judged by its cover.

But in a thousand everyday situations, we are obliged to do precisely that.

Do I dare tell her my secret? Do I dare buy his used car? Which of those unknown people at the party shall I approach? Is the man coming toward me on the pavement just an unusually happy citizen or a raving lunatic?

We often have no other basis apart from appearance and behavior to answer questions of that kind. It would, of course, be extremely comfortable if there were a few simple and reliable rules of thumb such as "men with close-set eyes are untrustworthy," or "sexually gifted women walk with their toes turned in." And most comfortable of all would be to have a scientific classification system that made it possible to draw definite conclusions from visible to invisible characteristics.

The Swiss Johann Caspar Lavater (1741–1801) tried to create a system of that kind. He started out from the face being the mirror of the soul, and considered that ability and personality found visible expression in the human body in the form of beauty. His *Physiognomische Fragmente* (1775–78) was full of flashes of genius, but also passing fancies and ancient prejudices. This mixture became tremendously popular at the end of the eighteenth century.

Lavater was far from alone in his belief that beautiful was good. Peter Camper, Charles White, and other early racial theorists also based their ideas on aesthetic criteria. The philosopher Christoph Meiners (1745–1810) in Gottingen divided humankind into two races: the beautiful and the ugly. Whites were the beautiful and had ability, courage, and a longing for liberty. And according to Meiners, the darker you were, the uglier, stupider, and more cowardly you also were.

Particularly striking was the contrast when Winckelmann's ideal Greek sculptures were being compared with real Africans living in misery. Lavater used a similar trick when he put idiots and blacks on the same footing, then contrasted them with major white geniuses.

Reason, Lavater said, denies the thought that a Leibniz or a Newton could be found in the body of an idiot, or that the man in the lunatic asylum could be a great mathematician. Would Leibniz have been able to find his philosophy in the skull of a Lapp? Would Newton have weighed the planets in the head of a Negro, "whose race is so impressed on his face, whose eyes bulge, whose lips, as swollen as they are, hardly cover his teeth, who is generally fleshy and round?"

To that question, naturally Lavater expected his readers to reply with a resounding no. But Lichtenberg answered "Yes, why not?"

The great aphorist Georg Christoph Lichtenberg (1742–99) was professor of physics at the University of Göttingen. Physicists had for centuries believed that the laws of beauty decided the orbits of the planets. As the circle was the most beautiful form, they believed the heavenly bodies must move in circles.

But now this old image of the universe had been toppled. Kepler and Newton had shown that the planets moved in ellipses totally independent of man's changing views on what was beautiful. Now Lavater appeared, attempting to use Newton's name to introduce into psychology the same unfounded belief in beauty that Newton had driven out of physics.

Lichtenberg considered that a backward step.

He also had personal reasons to distrust physiognomy, for he was scarred from smallpox and had a hunchback from illnesses and accidents in his childhood. So he asked himself why everything to be read in a face should only be about inborn ability and personality. "Why not then about the month of birth, cold weather, wet diapers, thoughtless nursemaids, damp bedrooms and childhood diseases?"

What really goes on when body and soul take on each other's forms? Lichtenberg asked in his pamphlet *Über Physiognomik* (1778). Is it the soul that shapes a body? And would it shape a similar one if it had a second chance? "Or does the soul fill the body like an elastic fluid which completely takes on the form of the vessel?"

If flat noses mean malice, does one become malicious from having one's nose flattened? A wise man may fall and become confused, and it has even happened that a crazy man has fallen and become wise—but with that they do not acquire a new profile, do they?

We often judge faces from the associations with which they provide us. We consider ugly a person resembling our enemy. The person who reminds us of someone we love we find beautiful. Pure chance influences the judgment.

It is very rash to attach facial similarities to those of character. What does the beauty of the body really say about that of the soul? "Is the flesh to pass judgement on the spirit?"

No, for in that case, little Lichtenberg, who was only 4 feet, eleven inches tall and had enormous flat feet would be judged beforehand. His own ugliness helped him see through Lavater's prejudices:

"Would Newton's soul be able to sit in a negro's skull? An angel's soul in a disgusting body? That's impossible, says the physiognomist. But you can always stop him with the simple question: 'Why not?' "

Lavater was stung. In the next edition, he changed his wording and instead asked whether Newton could have weighed the planets in the skull of a "Labrador Indian able to count only up to six."

It was fairly obvious that no one could do calculations without having learned to count. With that, Lavater had abandoned his main theme: that ability can be judged by appearances.

"Physiognomy" was a pseudoscience and has long since been abandoned. But the debate between Lichtenberg and Lavater is still topical, as all racism is a kind of "physiognomy."

From external characteristics—curly hair, black skin, thick lips—the racist draws conclusions on internal characteristics: stupid, lazy, unreliable. But with what right?

We all have a tendency to believe that noble features indicate a noble character, that a brutal appearance entails brutal behavior. On suppositions of that kind, at the end of the nineteenth century Cesare Lombrose (1836–1909) based a whole criminology. He believed that simply from appearances he could point out "the born criminal." There was no need to wait for someone of that kind to commit a crime.

It would be best to imprison that person directly, simply on appearance.

Nor does the racist care much about what has really happened, but judges by appearance. A person who looks like that, he thinks, cannot be a real person. But you can always stop him with the simple "Why not?"

Lichtenberg was not free of the prejudices of his day. Nor, for that matter, was Benjamin Franklin. Lichtenberg has said things about Jews, and Franklin about blacks, for which no one but God can forgive them. But on one point, Lichtenberg was long before his time: he questioned the supposed connection between appearance and personality, between race and genius.

For that insight, he had his own ugliness to thank.

Lichtenberg was so ugly that people backed away at the sight of him, and he saw in their eyes what they thought about him. He saw prejudices being born in them: Look at that ugly little thing. There can't be any thoughts in a skull like that.

"Why not?" replied Lichtenberg.

4

The Struggle Against the Slave Trade Begins

James Ramsay, 1784

THE SLAVES OF Greece and Rome were usually of the same race as their owners, so slavery never gave rise to racial prejudices. The Greeks met Africans largely on the battlefield and in the markets, where blacks were respected as dangerous opponents and cunning merchants.

The new slavery began when the death of American Indians created a shortage of labor in America. Over a few decades, the Indian population of the island of Hispaniola was decimated from about one million to only eleven thousand. Bishop Bartolomé de Las Casas, friend of the Indians, believed that freedom from forced labor would contribute to the survival of the remaining Indians. So he suggested that the Spanish colonists in the West Indies be allowed to import twelve black slaves each, and this was granted by the king.

That is how a trade that turned out to be extraordinarily profitable began. For 400 years, mainly British ships transported about fifteen million black forced laborers from Africa to America, and whole industries—the sugar industry in the West Indies, cotton production in the American South—were based entirely on forced labor. Slavery created racial prejudices against blacks and these prejudices in their turn came to motivate slavery. The vicious circle was reinforced when slavery began to be questioned in the late eighteenth century. To defend and justify the trade in human beings, a racist ideology was created that denied that blacks were human.

In his *History of Jamaica* (1774), Edward Long wrote that blacks stood lower than animals. They desired nothing else but to eat and drink, couple, and laze about. Perhaps they had once been human, but now they had sunk to a state of animal ignorance, idleness, and superstition. Through their bestial habits, their stupidity and depravity, they distinguished themselves from the rest of humankind; so no other conclusion was possible than that the Negro belonged to a different species from our own.

James Ramsay was one of the first to take up the fight against this growing racist ideology. He had served as a ship's doctor on a slave ship and never forgot what he saw. He stayed in the West Indies and was ordained there. As he was involved in the cause of the black people, he came into conflict with the plantation owners, and in 1781 was forced to return to his native country. In his book *An Essay on the Treatment and Conversion of African Slaves in the British Sugar Colonies* (1784), he examines the arguments of the British racists.

Certain characteristics are common to all human beings, says Ramsay. Others are common to all those with the same trade; others again to all those of the same race. Certain characteristics are common to the nations into which the races are divided, others to those who come from the same province or the same place, others again to those belonging to the same family. Among all these differences, why should just racial differences determine the value of a human being?

Racial differences are external and more visible than other group differences. It is easy to establish that the African has black skin and curly hair. But the conclusion cannot be drawn that this corresponds to internal differences. "As far as I can judge, there is no difference between the intellects of whites and blacks, but such as circumstances and education naturally produce."

We whites by no means lack experience of the blacks. We know that "their tongues are as musical, their hands as elegant and apt, their limbs as neatly turned, and their bodies as well formed for strength and activity as those of the white race."

A black houseboy can be as cunning and scheming as a European servant. The blacks have great abilities as storytellers and imitators. They are good mechanics, skilled lumbermen, and easily master the tasks they are given. As nurses they have a surprising ability to cure ordinary illnesses and often successfully tackle disorders that have baffled professional doctors.

I have, as a magistrate, heard black culprits wriggling their way round cross-examination by the prosecutor, Ramsay says. There was nothing in their mental equipment to distinguish them from Europeans or to indicate that they were of an inferior race.

"But the negroes have never created a polished society," the philosopher David Hume objects. Mr. Hume should be grateful he does not live in the days of Emperor Augustus. What civilization had the English created at that time? Had he lived only a thousand years ago, "his Northern pride, perhaps, would have been less aspiring and satisfied to have been admitted even on a footing of equality with the sable Africans."

The differences between countries existing today do not prove that the natives of a certain country have an innate inability for civilisation—but only that arts and sciences have arisen earlier in certain countries and climates than in others.

Why should the man who distinguishes himself from Mr. Hume through his flat nose have an innate inability to think? Mr. Hume is a large and bulky man—with the same justification, he could have maintained that nor would anyone without his size belly have his ability to think.

And even if the anatomists should one day show that one race thinks better than another, that does not prove that the more able have a right to buy and sell the less able.

Should it turn out that the races really are equipped differently, then that is no stranger than the fact that human beings of the same race are variously well-equipped to fulfill their tasks in society. The peasant cannot do the work of a mechanic, the mechanic cannot do that of the professor. But from that the conclusion does not need to be drawn that they belong to different species or have different kinds of souls—the peasant one soul, the professor another. No, on the contrary, societies become more flourishing the less such differences are emphasized, so that members of society can naturally dispose their abilities for their mutual benefit.

James Ramsay fought a lone battle for these ideas for many years in the West Indies. In England, he found Granville Sharp and some other like-minded people, who in 1787 founded the Abolition Society. The society succeeded only in effecting a parliamentary inquiry into the slave question before Ramsay died in 1789.

But the struggle he instigated went on, and twenty years after Ramsay's death, the Abolition Society achieved its aim. The slave trade was abolished in 1808 in England.

5

For Jews and Blacks

Henri Grégoire, 1789

One October day in 1789, in the midst of the storms of the French Revolution, a little Catholic priest from rural Lorraine rose to his feet in parliament and spoke for the Jews:

"For fifteen years I have studied the customs of this singular people," he said. "So I think I have the right to say that many of those who speak against the Jews do so with shameful irresponsibility."

The Jews constituted only a few per thousand of the population of France. But in Lorraine and other provinces bordering Germany, lived a great many poor Jewish rag-and-bone men and small traders. They were subject to severe special taxation, were not allowed synagogues, permitted to live only in certain streets, and became so isolated that most of them could neither speak nor read French. The hatred and contempt from those around them increased their isolation and reinforced their conservatism.

As there were no banks, the peasants were dependent on the Jews for minor credits while waiting for the harvest. For the aristocracy it was more convenient to impose extra taxes and dues on the hated Jewish moneylenders than to collect the taxes directly from the peasants. The taxes forced up interest rates, and with the high rates of interest as an excuse, the aristocracy imposed even higher taxes on the Jews. The anger of the peasants was directed not against the aristocracy, who took the money, but against the Jews, who collected it.

Henri Grégoire (1750–1831) was one of the first to realize how this worked. On the other hand, he did not understand either the significance of credit in the economy or the value of Jewish culture. His long-term program for the rehabilitation of the Jews involved removing them from the physically and morally destructive life of towns and forcing them to become smallholders, like those in Grégoire's own congregation.

The exodus was to break the power of the rabbis and ease the assimilation of the Jews into French society. Most of all, it was important that Jewish children went to the same schools as other children—that would soon make them into good Catholics and French citizens, which to Grégoire stood out as the natural aim for everyone living in France.

Grégoire had already promulgated this program before the revolution in *Essai sur la régénération physique, morale et politique des juifs* (1789). In parliament, he concentrated on the first and most important step: to procure citizens' rights for the Jews.

Opposition came from both the Catholic phalanx to which Judaism was a rival religion, and from the anti-Catholic phalanx who were against all forms of religion. Grégoire met their arguments in the following way:

> It is said that the Jews may not become citizens, because they are intolerant and superstitious, because they devote themselves to shameful professions such

as that of moneylender, because they are full of innate evil, because they lack patriotism for France . . .

Perhaps it is slightly difficult for anyone considered not to be a citizen of his native country to cherish the right patriotic feelings for it. And as far as professions are concerned, the Jews practiced every conceivable profession—in the days of Jesus. If that went well then, why not now?

Europe has created four hundred regulations to erect a wall between Jews and Christians. All nations have in vain united their forces to eradicate a people who exist in all nations. The bad qualities of the Jews are the inevitable consequence of the oppression to which they have been exposed.

You have declared sacred the rights of man and the citizen—remember, then, that the 50,000 Jews of this country are human and request that they also may become citizens.

That was how Henri Grégoire spoke.

He was an unusual priest. Son of a village tailor, born in the district where he became the parish priest, a keen educator who taught the peasants new agricultural techniques, Grégoire founded a parish library in which he read newspapers to his congregation after services.

He was elected to parliament and became one of the first to join the revolutionary forces. He used the prestige this brought him with great consistency and stamina to fight prejudice against Jews and black people.

In his 1784 essay, James Ramsay had also compared contempt for blacks with the contempt for Jews. It was, he said, the same mechanisms of exclusion functioning in both cases.

In Grégoire's writings, the parallel becomes even clearer. Both Jews and blacks were strangers from the other side of the

Mediterranean and were considered unsuitable for French citizenship. Just as the ghetto with its isolation and exclusion from professions had hindered the development of the Jews, so had slavery hindered that of the blacks. The animal ignorance and superstition both Jews and blacks were accused of were, to the extent that they existed at all, the result of oppression and misery.

A Christian should know that the soul has neither gender nor color and should beware of creating gratuitous differences between human beings, Grégoire said. Before God, we are all equal and so there is no reason to refuse Jews and blacks the same rights as other citizens.

These ideas had a great many enemies. When Grégoire was appointed bishop, word was spread around that he had been chosen with "Jewish votes," and his diocese was called "little synagogue." Not until after many months of delays and opposition did parliament finally decide on September 28, 1791, to award citizen's rights to a limited number of Jews in the northeastern provinces.

Local authorities continued to put every possible obstacle in the way of Jewish citizenship, exploiting the anticlerical laws of the revolution to banish Jews that they considered undesirable. Two things, however, were achieved—the special taxes on Jews were abolished, and Jews were allowed to live anywhere in France.

In 1794, Grégoire was also successful in driving through a law banning slavery throughout the entire French colonial empire. But powerful economic interests defied the ban and it did not last long. All his life, Grégoire continued his fight against the slave trade and racial prejudice.

The powerful of this earth have always attempted to

depict their power as the result of superior virtues and abilities, he wrote in *La noblesse de la peau* (1826). India has her caste system, feudalism has its aristocrats and our own day, colonial times, has "the aristocracy of skin."

The colonial laws put innumerable obstacles in the way of any mixing between black and white. From 1761, all personal files in the French colonies had to include the race of the person concerned. From 1773, children with a black mother and white father were not allowed to bear the father's name, but had to take a name that clearly showed on which side of the racial border they belonged. In 1779, blacks were forbidden to wear the same clothes as whites—even clothing had clearly to define their African origin. A black man who had a relationship with a white woman was sentenced to lose his male organ and to be hanged. In practice, the court contented itself occasionally by cutting off his ears and having him flogged. A white man who had a relationship with a black woman was to be fined a ton of sugar, but the sentence was never carried out.

Why were all these laws and punishments necessary if the superiority of the whites was so self-evident? Grégoire replied: the stated superiority is a prejudice—a faulty view that has been accepted without examination.

Other people's prejudices are easy to find. There are tribes in the interior of Africa who believe the Devil is white and consider the color of the white man's skin to be a result of disease. Our own prejudices, on the other hand, we do not see. We are blinded by ignorance, idleness, and arrogance, by passive belief in authority, and the desire to gain advantage at the expense of other people.

Grégoire remained a thorn in the flesh to the last. He went on criticizing Napoleon's dictatorship even when

Napoleon carried through the program for the rehabilitation of the Jews, which Grégoire had failed to get the national assembly to approve. He went on criticising the British occupation of Ireland, even when the British were in the lead over the abolition of the slave trade.

When the revolution's reign of terror demanded that he renounce his Catholic faith, he refused point blank. When the Catholic church demanded on his deathbed that he renounce the ideas of the revolution, he refused just as forcefully.

He did eventually receive Holy Communion. In 1831, twenty thousand people, many of them Jews and blacks, followed his coffin to the churchyard in Montparnasse.

6

Doctor in Africa

Thomas Winterbottom, 1803

"DARKEST AFRICA" WAS invented in the nineteenth century. Eighteenth-century Europeans knew more about Africa than most other parts of the world. Relatively speaking, knowledge was greater then than during any other period before the 1950s, Philip Curtin writes in *The Image of Africa* (1964).

From the Middle Ages until the seventeenth century, the lives of European peasants did not change very much. Similarly, the life of the African peasant was roughly the same from the Middle Ages up to the nineteenth century. Nor at the time were there great differences in living standards between European and African peasants.

The British trading with Africa in the eighteenth century were not particularly surprised by what they saw and seldom expressed any racial prejudices, Curtin says. Race was a mark identifying the group and was not regarded as a cause of the characteristics of the group.

When at the end of the eighteenth century racial prejudice began to manifest itself, it was first in statements about "the African" in general. Such generalizations were often in marked contrast to what was said about individual Africans. Individuals were human beings like everyone else and thus different from one another. "The African" on the other hand was always the same: an inhuman savage.

The majority of scholars who studied "the African" had never seen an African except as a corpse on the autopsy slab, or as an exhibit in a zoo, or possibly as a slave. The anthropologists did their research on alien peoples from their armchairs at home.

So it was a remarkable event when Thomas Winterbottom (1766–1859) published his book *An Account of the Native Africans in the Neighbourhood of Sierra Leone* (1803). It was, says Curtin, the first time an English scholar had published an ethnographical study based on field work. Winterbottom was so long before his time that he has not even been included in the history of anthropology.

Thomas Winterbottom was a young, newly qualified doctor when he went to Freetown in Sierra Leone to take charge of the health care of 1,131 freed American Negro slaves, a few hundred Europeans, and all the others who lived there around the river mouth.

When Winterbottom arrived, the situation was desperate—the colonists, black and white, were dying like flies, and he was himself attacked by malaria. Gradually, however, he managed to clear up the situation and halt the galloping mortality. But when the French fleet destroyed his surgery and his whole store of medicines in 1794, he returned to England.

With his book, he wanted to correct at least some of the false concepts of "the Negro" now spreading over Europe and used in defense of the slave trade. He turned against his medical colleague, Charles White, in particular, who in his book *An Account of the Regular Graduations in Man* (1799) had made a great many cocksure statements about black Africans—without ever having been to Africa.

According to White, the beauty of the white race is already evidence of its superiority. So Winterbottom began by describing the beauty of the inhabitants of Sierra Leone. They can be recognized by their smooth velvety skin. Both men and women are above European height, well-proportioned, lively, and open. The poise of the young women in particular is pleasing and free of restraint.

How then had the idea that Africans were ugly arisen? Well, pictures of human beings of an alien race try to maximize the features considered typical of that race. The model may be the attempt in Greek art to create a type, an ideal beauty, which perhaps never existed in any living person and which almost completely eliminates the various expressions of individual faces.

The wonderful diversity of feature in human beings and animals is reduced by Charles White to a matter of the angle between two lines in the profile. With the help of these angle measurements, White attempts to decide which rung the African has on the ladder of creation, and depreciates his claim to the dignity of man. But that judgment, Winterbottom says, is based on a series of false and misinterpreted observations.

White: A Negro's skull has a narrow frontal bone and the space inside the skull is smaller than in a European.

Winterbottom: There are major differences between various European skeletons, so it is not enough to compare a few individual Africans and Europeans, as the differences found may be wholly random.

White: Europeans sweat a great deal, while on the other hand "a drop of sweat is scarcely seen upon negroes," monkeys sweat even less and dogs not at all. So the Negro stands lower than the European.

Winterbottom: The observation is unfounded. When an African works in hot sun, floods of sweat pour down his body. Blacks and whites show the same variations: some sweat more, others less.

White: Menstruation is less troublesome to African women than it is to Europeans.

Winterbottom: That's true, but the same applies to healthy and robust English women who do physical labor out of doors. It is not race, but the work situation that makes their menstruation easier.

White: African women have long breasts because they usually fling the breast over the shoulder to infants they are carrying on their backs.

Winterbottom: I have never seen that and I think it would arouse as much surprise on the west coast of Africa as in England. Among the lower classes, pendulous breasts are as common in Europe as they are in Africa. This is due to malnourishment and the habit of breast-feeding children for a long time. In Europe, clothing prevents us from seeing this.

White: Black women give birth with less pain than white women, just as animals give birth more easily than human beings.

Winterbottom: I have been present at a great many difficult deliveries and found that in no way are they different from deliveries in England. I have seen English women give birth more easily than I have ever been present at in Sierra Leone, and on the other hand I have been present there at deliveries that have lasted for twenty-four hours and more.

White: In respects in which animals surpass human beings, the African also surpasses the European. This concerns their sense of smell, their sight and hearing and memory, and the ability to chew.

Winterbottom: White provides no evidence whatsoever for these statements, which I think are utterly unfounded. It is true that I occasionally noticed that black people were swifter than I was at spotting game in the forest; but practice makes perfect and the English sportsman similarly sees his prey long before other people have even reacted.

Point by point, Winterbottom questioned White's statements—for instance, that "the Negro" was insensitive to pain, that his brain and his blood were of a different color from that of the whites, that he had larger sexual organs and became sexually mature earlier, and so on. Winterbottom's investigations did not in any of these respects find any significant racial differences.

But who cared? People took no notice of bald facts. On the other hand, the legends of the black man's large penis and small brain flew on the wings of rumor. The inventions and lies that Winterbottom refuted during the nineteenth century grew into a world of myths in which the white race sought evidence of its superiority.

Thomas Winterbottom himself calmly went on practicing his profession. When he died at the age of ninety-three, he was Europe's oldest practicing doctor.

7

The Skull Measurer's Mistake

Friedrich Tiedemann, 1837

RACIST IDEOLOGY BEGAN to appear in the early nineteenth century primarily as a defense of the trade in slaves and then of slavery itself.

The English Anti-Slavery Society was formed in 1823, and after a ten-year struggle, succeeded in having slavery banned in the British colonies. That same year, 1833, the American Anti-Slavery Society was formed to fight against slavery in the United States. The slave owners needed a scientific theory that would make slavery appear natural and justified.

During the 1830s, the last remains of the almost eradicated Native American population were moved from the eastern states of the United States to camps on the other side of the Mississippi. The forced resettlement was conducted in an outrageously cruel fashion, and mortality, particularly among children and old people, was terrifyingly high. A scientific theory was needed to explain why these measures were necessary.

At the time, the races were classified according to color. But skin color was hard to measure. Though inborn, it is clearly influenced by external circumstances—even the whitest skin darkens in the rays of the sun. And, most of all, the causal connection between skin color and slavery was not entirely self-evident.

During the search for permanent and measurable race differences, scholars increasingly changed to examining the skulls of dead people. The skull could be weighed and measured, and was more permanent in size and shape than other parts of the body, both in life and after death. In addition, it was intuitively easy to presume that a causal connection could be found between the capacious cranium and civilized behavior.

So skulls were collected and measured.

The largest collection in the world—six hundred human skulls—was in Philadelphia and belonged to the American Samuel Morton (1799–1851). He came from a Quaker family with an Irish background and had studied medicine in Edinburgh and Paris. He started collecting skulls when he was twenty, and in his forties published two monumental volumes of prints, of which *Crania Americana* (1839) is the best known.

Morton's conclusion from his measurements was unambiguous: white people's skulls were largest, which gave them "decided and unquestionable superiority over all the nations of the earth." That was why they had spread all over the world. "In Asia, in Africa, in America, in the torrid and the frigid zones, have not all the other races of men yielded and given place to this one . . . ?"

Yes, indeed. And Morton had the explanation: large skull.

One hundred and thirty years later, another scientist, Stephen Jay Gould, set about examining and checking Morton's figures. He found that Morton had made a number of faulty calculations, insignificant in themselves, but systematic in the sense that they all contributed to support Morton's conclusion.

Morton based his conclusions on averages for different races. But represented among his 144 Indian skulls were many different Indian peoples whose skulls were in themselves of very different sizes. If these groups are not weighed, the number of skulls from a certain group would quite randomly influence the final result. That randomness also contributed to supporting Morton's conclusion.

But the determining factor was something else: namely, that the size of the head is related to the size of the body to which it belongs. Men have on an average larger bodies than women. So, if white men's skulls are compared with those of black women, then you can be quite sure the result will be that whites have larger skulls than blacks.

On the other hand, if in Morton's collection men are compared with men, and women with women, it can be seen that black men have slightly larger skulls than white men, while black women have slightly smaller skulls than white women.

Morton did not bother to distinguish between the sexes. By comparing the female skulls of small Hottentots with male skulls of large Englishmen, he "proved" that black people were stupid and inferior—which was what he wanted to prove.

Morton was not dishonest. He himself published all the raw data needed to establish which mistakes he made. But his scientific reputation was such that no one questioned his conclusion, discussed his methods, or even bothered to check the figures.

To Morton and his American contemporaries, the problem was not whether whites were or were not superior. Whites considered this as obvious as fresh butter is better than rancid. The problem was to measure this superiority. The point at issue was settled; what remained was to find a method to express that truth in figures.

They could not bring in body weight, for just as convincing as it seemed to maintain a connection between the skull and what is inside it, it would be just as ridiculous to maintain that intelligence was dependent on body weight. So no one paid any attention to the connection between the size of the body and that of the skull. No one, except Friedrich Tiedemann (1781–1861).

He came from Marburg in Germany. As a gynecological surgeon during the Napoleonic Wars, Tiedemann started studying the development of the skull of the fetus. In 1823, he became a professor in Heidelberg and continued his neurological studies, including some dolphins.

The study of dolphins taught Tiedemann that a small head can very well be combined with great intelligence. He also realized that an animal species that is "low" in the biological hierarchy can possess a far more complicated mental capacity than that of "higher" animal species.

In dolphins it was clear that the weight of brain varied with gender, body length, body weight, and acute body condition. The dolpins also taught Tiedemann not only to study averages in large groups, but also to take an interest in individuals and the variations between individuals as well as between groups and divisions of groups.

Tiedemann measured skulls by filling them with millet, then weighing the millet. The most capacious cranium in his collection—fifty-nine ounces—was from a Native American man. In second place came a white man with fifty-seven ounces. Third was an African, fourth a white, and fifth place was shared among three whites, a Mongol, and a Malay.

The most capacious female skull came from a Malay woman at forty-one ounces. A white and a Native American shared second place, and the third place was shared by one black and one white woman.

If, instead, the bottom placings are studied, fifteen percent of the Mongol skulls measured below the thirty-two-ounce level, together with thirteen percent of the Malayan and ten percent of the Native American. But only one single African and one single white measured below that level.

These results did not fit in with the current race hierarchy, in which whites were always to be at the top and blacks at the bottom. Tiedemann drew the conclusion that the anatomists and natural historians who ascribed to the African a smaller skull and smaller brain than the European and all other human races, were quite simply wrong.

As the human skulls were not accompanied by information on body length, body weight etc., then it was not clear what the figures really meant. Perhaps they entailed nothing more than that human beings of certain races are larger or better nourished than others, which does not necessarily influence intelligence.

And what quantity of brain matter was really necessary in order to be a human being? Was any more needed than we all had by nature? On the basis of his investigations, Tiedemann maintained that as far as the brain matter needed for mental faculties was concerned, nature had "equipped people of all the human races equally."

Tiedemann's researches had great influence in Europe and contributed to delaying the advance of racism.

Tiedemann had three sons who participated in the German revolution of 1848—one of them was executed by firing squad and the other two fled to America. There their father's research had not had the same impact as it had had in Europe. America believed Morton. His teachings on the inferiority of the colored races were scientifically inferior to Tiedemann's, but they filled a deeply felt need in white Americans.

The same year that Tiedemann died, 1861, Sanford B. Hunt summarized Morton's teaching as follows:

> In history, we find that, so far as the welfare of nations is concerned, there is no such thing as equality; that the strong hand, guided by the intelligent brain, has ever conquered. So the small-brained South American Indians were driven out by the larger-brained North American Indians, who then in their turn were driven to their forest graves by Teutons with even larger brains. It was not conquest or subjugation, but annihilation.

In this race struggle, the "Indian" and the "Negro," according to Morton, were born losers. Nature had condemned them to be exterminated and enslaved. So racists, whatever violence they committed, were essentially innocent. Morton's teaching, as opposed to Tiedemann's, fulfilled the main task of a racist ideology: to justify violence against other races.

8

Poet Astray

William Howitt, 1838

After the Napoleonic Wars, in 1815, Great Britain stood out as the military and industrial superpower. The English also very much wanted their country to be the moral example for other nations—roughly as the Americans did in the 1900s. And just as in our day, there were rebellious spirits who questioned the superpower and demanded that it should live up to its stated morality.

What we would today call a Third World perspective became particularly noticeable during the 1830s. The decade started with Bannister's fiery accusation of extermination policies in South Africa and Australia. He wrote in his *Humane Policy* (1830): "It is impossible to justify our present course of destroying everywhere those, whose only crime is that they precede us in the possession of lands, which we desire to enjoy to their exclusion."

A few years later John Howison published his critical colonial history Beannister published *European Colonies,* (1834), and the same year Herman Merivale gave his fierce Oxford lectures on "Colonization and Colonies." The 1837 parliamentary committee published frightening findings on the treatment of the natives in British possessions, and the Aborigines Protection Society was formed to halt future extermination of native peoples.

Of all those who at this time attacked European colonialism in general and the British in particular, no one was more eloquent than the English poet William Howitt.

"The object of this volume," he wrote in *Colonization and Christianity* (1838), "is to lay open to the public the most extensive and extraordinary system of crime which the world ever witnessed. It is a system which has been in full operation for more than three hundred years and continues yet in unabating activity of evil.

"The whole field of un-Christian operations in which this country, more than any other, is engaged, has never yet been laid in a clear and comprehensive view before the public mind."

We call those who inhabit other continents "heathens" and "barbarians." But how is it that these tribes know us? Chiefly by the very features that we attribute to them. They know us by our crimes and our cruelty. It is we who are, and must appear to them, the savages.

The barbaric acts of violence people who call themselves Christians have committed all over the world "are not to be paralleled by any other race however fierce, untaught and reckless of mercy and of shame, in any age of the earth," says Howitt.

Then he devotes 500 pages to an indignant account of acts of violence against indigenous peoples, from the Spanish conquest of the New World to the cruelties that the parliamentary committee had just described.

And he ends:

> Go, indeed, into any one spot, of any quarter of the world, and ask—no, you need not ask, you shall hear of our aggression from every people that know us.
>
> Many are the evils that are done under the sun; but there is and can be no evil like that monstrous and earth-encompassing evil, which the Europeans have committed against the Aborigines of every country in which they have settled. And in what country have they not settled?
>
> The cause of the Aborigines is the cause of three-fourths of the population of the globe. The evil done to them is the great and universal evil of the age, and is the deepest disgrace of Christendom.

Well said. But there is something in his tone of voice which does not really inspire confidence.

His affected rhetoric reminds me of how our 1990s reactionaries sounded in the 1970s, when they had the same blind faith in the Socialist Revolution as they have today in the Market. One wonders what happened to the young Howitt and all his ardor when the wind changed, as it always does, and blew in the opposite direction?

A torrent of poems, essays, novels, children's books, and translations continued to pour out of the workshop of William Howitt and his wife Mary. The couple learned Scandinavian languages in Germany, and Mary became Hans Christian Andersen's and Fredrika Bremer's English translator. This Nordic involvement gradually resulted in a major two-volume history of literature, *The Literature and Romance of Northern Europe* (1852).

The account of Scandinavian literature by the Howitts begins with a hymn of praise to the world power of Great Britain. The British fleet is everywhere; the sons of England are the rulers of the East, the West, and the South, pouring over the vast plains of America and Australia and taking possession of them.

Fourteen years earlier, William Howitt had seen this British expansion as a worldwide crime. Now he was reversing his view and only asking from where the British had found such strength for expansion.

By then it was agreed to seek the explanation for the British success in their "blood," their "race," in their biological heritage. Most considered it was Anglo-Saxon blood performing these miracles. But the Howitts did not think so: "Had [the blood] of Germany predominated we should have been now as Germany is, a country without colonies, without conquests, without a fleet, and without political liberty."

No, it is their Scandinavian heritage the British have to thank for their strength, their spirit of enterprise and their instinct to colonize. Their ancestors of ancient Scandinavia had a boundless love of war and seafaring. As the Vikings often took their women with them on their voyages, the children were literally born on the battlefield and grew up surrounded by weapons and bloodshed.

Fighting was part of their religion. Only those killed in battle would go to heaven, Valhalla, while those who died in their beds were to descend to hell. In their eyes, war and plundering expeditions were nothing criminal but, on the contrary, the most honorable activity to which a man could devote himself.

Although the English have now lived for eight hundred years under the influence of a religion that teaches the absolute opposite, the martial fire in their veins has not been extinguished. The same love of military honor, the same passion for discovering new countries, the same irresistible desire to conquer and colonize them, the same victorious ability to subdue large populations and savage nations still distinguishes the British from all other peoples.

"America, Australia, the Indies East and West, South Africa . . . and the isles of many a distant sea bear testimony to the survival of the spirit of the Vikings in the bosoms of the British."

Indeed—William Howitt had floated a long way on the current of time. He no longer spoke for the conquered and the subjugated. Now he saw history from the conqueror's point of view. The same conquests that fourteen years earlier he had indignantly condemned, he now praised as his country's greatest exploits. The same crude violence that he had branded in European behavior on other continents, he now sees as the flower of Scandinavian humanity and the engine of history.

Such things happen. They happened not only to William Howitt, but also to a great many others over those years. They went with their times, and those times took them more and more deeply into the darkness of the "blood."

9

The Three Races of America

Alexis de Tocqueville, 1840

"AT THE END of the year 1831, I found myself on the left bank of the Mississippi in a place the Europeans call Memphis."

It was in the depths of winter, and that year the cold was unusually severe, the ground a frozen crust and great ice floes on the water. A band of Indians was trying to make its way across to the other side of the river, where the government had promised them refuge. They had their families with them and were carrying their injured and sick, new-born infants, and dying old people. They had neither tents nor wagons, only weapons and a few supplies.

"I saw them go on board and the dismal sight will never leave my memory. No sobs could be heard, no laments. They were silent. Their misfortunes had already continued for so long that they seemed to them inescapable.

"The Indians had already boarded the boats that were to take them across; left on the shore were their dogs. When the animals realized the boats were about to disappear for good, they let out the most terrible howls, threw themselves into the icy waters of the Mississippi and swam after their masters."

The young French aristocrat Alexis de Tocqueville (1805–59) gives this on-the-spot account from his journey in America. He had been sent out to study American prisons, but his interest lay in the whole American social experiment. At the time, the United States was the only country trying to combine liberty and equality within the framework of a democratic form of government. Liberals from all over the world went there to study the American model.

But Tocqueville was soon made aware that liberty and equality concerned only one of America's three races. Indians and black people were kept outside democracy.

Blacks have lost the language, religion, and customs of their forefathers without having gained any new European culture. They have become suspended between two societies, "sold by the one and rejected by the other," Tocqueville writes.

"Negroes" have lost the right to their own person and cannot decide over their own lives without committing some kind of theft. Ever since birth, they have been told that their race is by nature inferior to the white race—they have almost begun to believe it themselves and are ashamed of being black. If it were possible, they would with joy relinquish being what they are.

White Americans on the other hand are proud of themselves and their race. They are united by a tremendous arrogance and not far from regarding themselves as belonging to a special species apart from other humanity.

This applies particularly to the Americans of the South, who from birth have dictatorial authority over their surroundings; their first impression of life is that they are born to command, for black adults obey their slightest whim without resistance.

One needs only to read the race laws of the South to realize what a desperate situation both races find themselves in, Tocqueville goes on to say. Teaching a black man to read or write entails severe punishment. He is kept as near to the level of animals as possible.

As soon as the blacks become free people, they will protest that they have no rights as citizens. As they are not allowed to be equals to the whites, they will become their enemies.

The whites of the South are infinitely superior in resources, but the blacks are superior in numbers and driven to despair. What will be the fate of the whites? The same as that of the Moors in Spain?

After having ruled the country for centuries, perhaps they will be forced to retreat and hand the country over to the blacks. That danger might be distant, but it haunts the American consciousness like a bad dream.

For the Indian, this bad dream is already reality. The Indians have the same arrogance as the whites and are full of fantasies about their noble origins. They do not seek to imitate us. On the contrary, they see barbarism as a distinction and reject civilization, perhaps not from hatred of it, but from fear of being like us.

"These savages have not just retreated," Tocqueville writes, "they have been annihilated."

"It is easy to establish with which methods this annihilation has worked," he goes on. "I would not wish the reader to think I am exaggerating. Much of what I speak of I have seen with my very own eyes."

The Indians are robbed of their property with perfectly

normal and, so to speak, lawful methods. When the European population approaches an area in which Indians live, the U.S. government sends an ambassador, who tries to persuade and bribe the Indians to move farther away. If they hesitate, the ambassador then points out to the Indians that pressure from the white man is great and the government will soon no longer be able to guarantee their safety.

The Indians then move to new wildernesses farther away. Ten years later, the Europeans have caught up with them and it starts all over again.

"In this way, the Americans acquire at bargain prices whole provinces which even the richest rulers of Europe would not be able to afford," says Tocqueville.

Whichever way one regards the fate of the North American natives, this evil appears to be inevitable. If the savages stay, they are driven out. If they try to become civilized, they are exposed to oppression and wretchedness. "If they continue to wander from wilderness to wilderness, they will perish. If they try to stay, they will also perish."

Despite their shameful atrocities, the Spaniards never succeeded in exterminating the Indian race. But the Americans in North America have achieved that aim without effort—calmly, lawfully, humanely, without spilling blood, and, in the eyes of the world, not offending a single one of their high moral principles.

"Without spilling blood" was certainly not true of the North American massacres of Native Americans. Tocqueville is describing the self-image of whites. His words are ambiguous—the depth of his irony does not appear until he finally summarizes the American ability to exterminate people with good conscience in these words: "With greater respect for the laws of humanity, no one could have annihilated these people."

Although his journey lasted nine months, his book about the journey took eight years to write. The second part of *On Democracy in America* came out in 1840. Tocqueville's journey to Africa the following year has not had equal fame, but the Swedish writer Anders Ehnmark has shown that it was just as interesting.

The day after his arrival in Algeria, Tocqueville sets off into the interior. "Excellent road which appears to lead to the provinces of a vast empire but which one cannot take for more than twelve kilometres without having one's head chopped off," he notes.

"From up in Kouba we see Mitidja: a magnificent plain, twenty kilometres wide, 120 kilometres long, a whole province. Resembles Alsace. Green, but not a house, not a tree, nor a human being . . . wilderness." He at once thinks of the United States and the frontier. Here is unbroken soil, as in America. "A promised land, if it were not that it has to be cultivated with rifle in hand"—as in America.

France had lost its first empire in the New World. Now the French had spent ten years conquering a new empire in Africa. The thinking was that virgin soil was awaiting landless French people.

But the country was not empty. What was to be done with those already living there? The French had the American example before them. The Bedouins were compared with the Indians, and according to newspaper reports, they would "disappear" by themselves:

"Once the French have colonised Algeria, what happened to the redskins when pioneers colonised America will also happen to the Bedouins: they will disappear from the face of the earth," stated *Courrier de la Gironde* on June 11, 1846.

Some newspapers maintained that it was best to help nature along by killing the Arabs. Others thought the natives should be deported to the deserts of the interior. For those methods, there were also American prototypes.

Tocqueville took a verbal stand against genocide, but as a responsible politician—he was Minister for the Colonies at the time—he supported French Army terror as it razed villages, burnt crops and deported the inhabitants.

In Africa, Tocqueville is no longer seeking the conditions for liberty, but conditions for bondage, Ehnmark writes in *The Palace* (1990)—bondage as the prerequisite for a lasting French empire overseas.

The man who had been recently writing about the justice of "a people's struggle to free themselves from the yoke of another people," was now absorbed in how to increase the pressure on the yoke. How did that hang together?

Tocqueville could not explain. The only conceivable explanation—that the right to liberty of the weaker race had to give way to the right to expansion of the stronger—he never put into words. Was it too evident? Or too repelling?

The Scottish anatomist Robert Knox was not so squeamish. In his book *The Races of Man* (1850), he accepts European expansion even at the expense of the physical extinction of all colored races. He dismisses international law as a bad joke. "Laws are made to bind the weak, to be broken by the strong," he writes. "The only real right is physical force."

Could we really expect that mighty France would be content being "cribbed up, cabined and confined"—remaining within the boundaries chance and fortunes of war had allocated her? No, of course not.

And all this, even if France were regarded as but a nation. If regarded from a more elevated viewpoint and remembering that France represents a race, then we realize that the French claims are utterly justified. "Men of the Celtic race demand for their inheritance a portion of the globe equal to their energy, their numbers, their civilisation and their courage."

Knox shamelessly put into words the unspoken value premises underlying Tocqueville's African policies. Robert Knox and Arthur de Gobineau have both been called "the father of modern racism." In actual fact, racism had been practiced, defended, and questioned long before Knox and Gobineau. But Gobineau (1816–82) was one of racist ideology's first theorists—just as Tocqueville was one of democracy's.

Strangely enough, they were friends. As a young man, Gobineau had served as Tocqueville's secretary for a time. Their correspondence continued throughout their lives. With his *Essai sur l'inégalité des races humaines* (Essay on the Inequality of Human Races) Gobineau wished to create an equivalent and antithesis to his friend's *De la démocratie*. A thousand invisible threads connect the two works.

Knox accepted European expansion even when it entailed the extinction of the colored races. Gobineau instead considered that it would lead to the extinction of the Aryan races by mixing their blood with that of the conquered races.

He believes that when Aryan blood has been thinned out, the idea of equality soon arises and gradually healthy racial prejudices are lost, democracy becomes the natural form of government and leads to a levelling that makes all human greatness impossible.

As Aryan blood degenerates, strength, beauty, and intellect will disappear and humanity will be destined for moral and physical destruction. "What is terrible is not death but the certainty that we cannot attain it without first being degraded," Gobineau ends.

Hatred of democracy and equality in Gobineau is even more fundamental than hatred of colored people and aliens. Naturally, Tocqueville could not accept Gobineau's theses. "Can't you see the evil born from a doctrine that teaches that inequality is eternal—arrogance, violence, contempt for other people, tyranny and submission in all its forms?" he wrote to his friend.

In Europe, Knox and Gobineau were regarded as strange creatures. Another half century was to pass before Gobineau became a success in Germany. But from the very start he was received more positively by the American racists.

10

The Myth of the Anglo-Saxon Master Race

Charles Anderson, 1850

I do not know much about Charles Anderson. I cannot find him in the reference books. All I know is that he lived from 1814 to 1895 and was a politician in Ohio in the mid-1800s. He was one of the few who had the courage to oppose the fashionable political philosophy of the day—the theory of the Anglo-Saxon master race and its alleged mission in the world.

The history of the United States during its first sixty years (1789–1849) is a history of uninterrupted expansion. The original thirteen states on the American East Coast had expanded to become states and territories all over the continent. The continental expansion was completed with the war against Mexico in 1847–48. Mexico lost over half its territory to the United States. The areas that later became California, Nevada, Utah, Arizona, New Mexico, Texas, and parts of other states were taken from Mexico and incorporated into the United States.

Under the influence of this expansion, the American view of themselves and their role in the world changed.

Americans have always thought of themselves as a people with a special mission. The seventeenth-century Puritan settlers wished to create a society based on a religious vision. The eighteenth-century founding fathers wished to implement Enlightenment ideas of liberty and equality. These visions were never abandoned and lived on even during the period of expansion.

But ideas of equality were pushed further and further into the background and forward came a new ideology emphasizing the biological superioriy of the Anglo-Saxon race and its "manifest destiny"—its obvious task, its calling, its mission to conquer the continent.

Racism has been often depicted as a European invention. But Reginald Horsman studied the idea of a master race in the United States and considers that the American racists were in the lead. In the United States during the period 1830–50, white racial superiority was established as a "scientific fact." Faith in an Anglo-Saxon master race was accepted in leading American journals, standard works, and school textbooks.

The novelist Willian G. Simms spoke for many when just before the Mexican war he called for Americans to "obey our destiny and blood." In 1847 he wrote: "War is the greatest element of modern civilisation and our destiny is conquest. Indeed, the moment a nation ceases to extend its sway it falls a prey to an inferior but more energetic neighbour."

The nearest "inferior" neighbor was Mexico. Of the country's seven million inhabitants, six million are Indians and mixed races, wrote the American minister in Mexico City, Waddy Thompson. Like many others at the time, he found it easy to believe that millions of people in some mysterious way would simply cease to exist. "That the Indian race of Mexico must recede before us is quite as certain as that that is the destiny of our own Indians."

There was no need for any further discussion on whether American expansion should end at the Rio Grande, for "it will not," said politician William Brown from Indiana.

The most serious objection to these plans for expansion was that they would lead to a mixing of the races if the victors did not completely exterminate the vanquished.

"Extermination and acquisition must go together," said James Pollock of Pennsylvania on January 26, 1847. "Are we prepared for this? Are we prepared to make the war a war of races, and not stay our hand until every Mexican is driven from the land of his fathers?"

And from a purely practical point of view, how was this to be done? "A war of extermination is not necessary," stated *Merchants Magazine* in 1855, as already through their commercial strength, the superior races will appropriate most of the foodstuffs. This would bring about "the extinction in future times of all the barbarous races."

That is how politicians spoke and editors wrote, and they had the support of the science of the day. The sociologist George Fitzhugh published his *Sociology for the South* in 1854, five years before Darwin's *Origin of Species*. But he already saw it as a natural law that wherever the English and Americans settled among inferior races, they soon become the owners of the land and "gradually exterminate the original owners or force them into poverty." Nature itself authorizes, indeed, forces the stronger race to oppress and exterminate the weaker.

A leading American ethnographer, E. G. Squier, wrote in his book *Notes on Central America* (1855) that the secret behind the United States' success was the racial purity of the population.

Progress in the United States, he believed, was due to the rigid and

> inexorable refusal of the dominant Teutonic stock to debase its blood, impair its intellect, lower its moral standard, or peril its institutions by intermixture with the inferior and subordinate races of man.

The only hope for Central America is to change the composition of the population so that the white element becomes dominant. The natives must, as has already occurred in North America, leave room for

> . . . higher organisations and superior life.
>
> Short-sighted philanthropy may lament, and sympathy drop a tear as it looks forward to the total disappearance of the lower forms of humanity, but the laws of Nature are irreversible. Deus vult,—it is the will of God!

The most authoritative scientific expression of the American doctrine of the master race appears in Nott and Gliddon's great reference book *Types of Mankind* (1854). According to the authors, "Nations and races, like individuals, each have an especial destiny: some are born to rule and others to be ruled . . ." That is how far things had now gone from the starting point of the American constitution: that all men are born equal.

"No two distinctly marked races can dwell together on equal terms. Some races, moreover, appear destined to live and prosper for a time, until the destroying race comes, which is to exterminate and supplant them."

The superior race improves the world by conquering and annihilating the lower races standing in its way: "Human progress has arisen mainly from the war of the races. All the great impulses which have been given to it from time to time have been the results of conquests and colonizations."

One of the few scholars to go against the tide was the eighty-six-year-old Albert Gallatin, famous linguist and ethnologist. In his pamphlet *Peace with Mexico* (1847), Gallatin condemned the U.S. policy of conquest. With no valid reason to go to war against Mexico, the Americans had invented a very strange argument, Gallatin wrote. It stated that the people of the United States had an inherited, racial superiority that gave them the right to rule over the inferior Mexicans.

As a democracy, the United States had already rejected the old aristocracy's claim to an inherited right to rule. How then could the Americans as a people plead for such rights? How could their dubious descent from a few people called Angles and Saxons who had lived a thousand years ago, give them the right to rule over others, people living today? asked Gallatin.

Charles Anderson expressed it even more clearly in *An Address on Anglo-Saxon Destiny* (1850). The entire American people, regardless of party, has abandoned itself to a sentiment "which is a fallacy in philosophy, an untruth in history, and a gross impiety in religion"—namely the belief that Anglo-Saxons are superior to other races and therefore have been chosen by God for special works.

Is there such a thing as an Anglo-Saxon race? Anderson asks. Tacitus mentions neither Saxons nor Angles. The English of today are quite simply not Anglo-Saxons; they are also

Scots, Irish, and Welsh. The British-American people on both sides of the Atlantic are perhaps the most mixed, mongrel and heterogeneous stock of people on earth." Historical circumstances, not innate superiority or divine tasks, have put this people into the position to carry out some great things. But in other respects, in art and music, for instance, the accomplishments of the Anglo-Saxons are not overwhelming.

Many peoples have considered themselves born with the right to rule over others. Egyptians, Jews, Assyrians, Babylonians and Persians—they were all convinced that they had a mission of that kind. We ought to learn from their self-deception by seeing through our own, says Charles Anderson. All those deceived nations have been defeated and the same will happen to the American nation if it continues along its criminal path of conquest.

11

Let the Chinese Come!

Raphael Pumpelly, 1870

A GREAT MANY people did not think American expansion would stop at the Pacific Coast, but expected it to continue to the other side of the ocean.

As early as 1846, Senator Thomas H. Benton foresaw a future colonization of Asia. Anglo-Saxons and Celts, who had been given the divine task of conquering and replenishing the earth, would be "the reviver and regenerator of the inferior and torpid yellow people." Just how this rejuvenation was to occur in more practical terms remained unclear.

Other people believed that the yellow race could not be resuscitated, but was doomed to the same fate as the North American Indian: "The extinction of the red race upon this continent may be said to be almost consummated," wrote *The Democratic Review* in April 1850. "China, which by a sort of instinct, excluded the whites for thousands of years, is now open to a similar influence, and a crisis is reached in the history of the dark species of man."

The superior American race, *De Bow's Review* stated in 1852, would achieve world dominion and replace all other peoples. That had already occurred as far as the Pacific Coast. Now the process was continuing in Mexico, South America, and Asia. Wherever the Americans went, the inferior native population was gradually replaced by the higher race, obeying the great law that says that with contact between higher and lower races, the lower vanishes.

That was what the racists expected. The Aryan tribes that once left their ancestral home in Central Asia to journey in the direction of the sun and become first Europeans and then North Americans, would, they thought, continue to follow the sun and eventually return home after having conquered the entire world.

Raphael Pumpelly made this journey around the world, returning with a quite different conclusion.

His journey began at Harvard, where he was a professor. In 1860, he went west to take up the post of head of a large silver mine in Arizona. This was before the days of the transcontinental railway, and transport was by diligence over sixteen days with no sleep and the constant risk of being attacked by Indians or robbers. Naturally, Pumpelly is prepared to defend himself, but he also regards Indians as human beings and condemns the ruthless extermination policy to which they are being subjected.

> If it is said that the Indians are treacherous and cruel, scalping and torturing their prisoners, it may be answered that there is no treachery and no cruelty left unemployed by the whites. Poisoning with strychnine, the wilful dissemination of smallpox, and the possession of bridles, braided from the hair of scalped victims and decorated with teeth knocked

> from jaws of living women—these are heroic facts among many of our frontiersmen.

After a few years in Arizona, he goes on to Asia and becomes a mining engineer with first the Japanese and then the Chinese government. Among foreigners in China, he finds prejudices and race hatred based on lack of knowledge.

> The average foreigner in China, being wholly ignorant of everything connected with the history, social organization, and even the true character of the people, look down upon them . . . The more ignorant the foreigner, the more proudly he sees in himself the representative of the science, the intellectual refinement and material progress of the west. To this man the teeming population around him is simply a swarm of chattering animals . . .

Pumpelly himself had arrived at a different evaluation. The Chinese constitute a third of humankind, he writes. They live in an area that is not much greater than the United States east of the Mississippi *(sic)*. Through extraordinary industry, talent, and skill, these four hundred million people have managed to survive in their insufficient land area.

The walls keeping the Chinese inside China are now being pulled down. The need for labor on the other side of the ocean has lured many Chinese to travel to the United States. When they return, they spread to millions of Chinese their story of high wages and adventures in a foreign country.

If immigration from China is not stopped, it will increase. If it is encouraged, it will become enormous.

The Chinese in the United States still lack rights as citizens. They are degraded and despised, called idol worshippers, and accused of all kinds of vices. For this reason, the Chinese feel they have no future in the United States, so, as Pumpelly says, "seek California, as the pearl-diver does the bottom of the sea."

But if the Chinese were treated in the same way as other immigrants, then they would stay and make their home in the United States. If the same percentage of China's population as Germany's immigrated to the United States, we would have an influx of a million Chinese a year. Everything speaks for that being an advantage to the United States.

In the first generation alone, the Chinese make a greater contribution to the prosperity of America than other immigrant groups. It is the Chinese who are building the transcontinental railway. They cultivate hitherto unused land. They save on raw materials, and through competition force even us to be thrifty. They are already working in all trades. After a few years, the worker's small savings have grown and the coolie becomes a capitalist. No other people is so inclined as the Chinese to accumulate capital and give their children an education.

But will the Chinese then not drive white Americans out of the market? Yes, to the extent that they are more efficient than we are—and through their efficiency alone, they have proved their right to citizenship.

What Pumpelly suggested was the opposite of the dream of the white racists. It was not China that was to be colonized by American settlers; the already overpopulated China, on the contrary, was to colonize the Western United States, just as Europe had colonized the East Coast.

What happened?

The first 325 Chinese arrived in the United States during the California gold rush in 1849. That year, 100,000 people came to San Francisco. But it was the 325 Chinese who gave cause for anxiety.

During the 1850s, 2.5 million people emigrated from Europe and only 35,000 from China. But it was the Chinese immigration that was considered a threat.

When Pumpelly's book *Across America and Asia* came out in 1870, the United States had accepted nearly 200,000 Chinese immigrants, of which the majority had already returned to China. The Chinese formed less than two per cent of the population of the United States. And yet words such as "landslide" and "floods" were used.

Why? One explanation is that nearly all the Chinese went to the same state, California. At the time, they constituted ten per cent of the population and almost a quarter of the labor force. That was conspicuous.

A third of California's whites came from the Southern states, a majority of the others from other states in the West. Their attitudes toward African Americans and Native Americans defined the norm for how to treat minorities. The Chinese were the largest minority and so were the worst affected.

The first anti-Chinese riot occurred in the gold rush year of 1849 and race riots with mob violence, killings, and arson recurred later at intervals of a few years. In 1854, the Chinese found themselves with no legal protection against such attacks because they had lost the right to testify in court. The California Supreme Court's motivation was clearly racist—the Chinese were said to belong to "a people whose mendacity is well known, a race inferior by nature."

The press, of course, went even further. "It is my deliberate opinion that the Chinese are, morally, the most debased people on the face of the earth," the influential journalist Bayard Taylor wrote in 1855.

Medical science added its straw to the stack. Arthur B. Stout's report *Chinese Immigration* (1862) is a fantastic potpourri of medical and ethnographical fantasies. The Chinese constituted a threat primarily through inherited diseases that were the result of centuries of vice and impossible to treat with western medicine.

In a later report, he maintained that it would be better for the United States to be devastated by Genghis Khan's hordes than to allow Chinese immigrants to "insiduously poison the wellsprings of life"—presumably by mixing their genes with those of the rest of the American population.

In 1870, when Pumpelly's book came out, the transcontinental railway had just been completed and 15,000 Chinese railroaders became unemployed. At the same time huge numbers of workers arrived from the East on the new railway. Outbreaks of anti-Chinese violence became more and more common. In 1871, the first lynchings of Chinese occurred, and in Los Angeles twenty-two Chinese were killed, while hundreds were made homeless.

The Chinese withdrew into their "Chinatowns." The Chinese quarters became a kind of ghetto built into fortresses with self-defense and fire brigades. Many Chinese lived their whole lives in America, not daring to go outside the relative security of the Chinatowns.

In 1873, the wave of speculation on the New York Stock Exchange dipped and panic broke out. In California, the depression deepened and 100,000 people became unemployed.

Employers with Chinese employees received threatening letters. Special anti-Chinese trade unions such as "United Brothers of California" were formed. Many small towns burned down their Chinese quarters and forced the Chinese out. In 1876, after a severe drought had destroyed California's crops and the anti-Chinese "Working Man's Party" had won a third of the seats in the state assembly, the time had come for a federal inquiry to look more closely into the "Chinese problem."

The inquiry really needed only to read the reference books. In *Cyclopaedia of Political Science* (1881–1888), Emile Montegut established that history in the correct sense of the word belonged only to the white race, which has taken possession of the earth. There is no greater obstacle to development of true civilization than the yellow races. The yellow people have always played an accidental and fatal part in history. The yellow people believe in nothing except force. The sabre driven into the ground and worshipped by the hordes of Attila is their real god.

Wherever the yellow people pass, life dries up and becomes extinct. Their civilization rapidly attains its limit and never renews itself, Montegut wrote.

Henry George, on the other hand, under the heading "Chinese Immigration" rejected the idea that the Chinese constituted an inferior race. But, in his eyes, this made them even more dangerous. Chinese immigration should be banned because it would lead to a "Mongolization" of America. Previously, brute strength had been how one population had replaced another. Instead, it is now the ability to work for low pay and live simply.

"Just as the Saxon supplanted the Briton on English soil, or the white race has supplanted the Indian race on this continent, so may the Chinese, if free play be allowed their immigration, supplant the white race."

The politicians listened. In 1882, Chinese immigration was halted by the "Chinese exclusion act." The new laws released a flood of race riots leading to the death of twenty-two Chinese in Rock Springs. Violence then spread all along the West Coast: the Chinese in Pasadena, Hollister, Redding, Los Angeles and twenty-four other towns were hunted like animals and many were killed. Tacoma, Wash., Santa Rosa, Calif., and thirty-five other towns drove out their Chinese immigrants altogether.

In 1892, Congress closed the last loophole in the anti-Chinese laws. Chinese with no identity cards were immediately deported. American legislation infected South Africa, Australia, New Zealand, and Canada, which all drew up similar anti-Chinese laws.

Pumpelly's dream of an America that would unite China with Europe was crushed. Racism victoriously advanced in a world that was growing darker.

12

Exterminating People Is Wrong

Langfield Ward, 1874

In 1874, with an obscure country publisher in England, an obscure man called Langfield Ward brought out a small, obscure pamphlet that even in its day aroused no attention at all. It was called *Colonialization in Its Bearing on the Extinction of the Aboringinal Races*, and asked the question: Has Europe the right to exterminate the natives of other continents?

Bartolomé de Las Casas (1474–1566) had asked the same question shortly after the discovery of the New World. Since then, the question had come to be regarded as increasingly old-fashioned, ignorant, and irrelevant. "Extermination," "eradication,""annihilation," were already accepted phenomena, fashionable concepts in the discussions of the day in English, German, and French.

How had this come about?

In 1796, a young French anatomist George Cuvier proved that whole species of animals, even animals as large as the mammoth and the mastodon, could die out, and had died out. Cuvier, a child of the French Revolution, believed that the animal species had become annihilated through some vast catastrophes, which he called "revolutions of the earth."

The father of British geology, Charles Lyell, did not experience the siege of the Bastille, but the Industrial Revolution in England. He saw society becoming fundamentally reshaped through small, gradual changes, and thought the same thing happened in nature—an animal species dies out just as a firm goes bankrupt when it cannot adapt to changed circumstances in the market.

Charles Darwin read Lyell's newly published book *Principles of Geology* (1832) on his way across the Atlantic on the *Beagle*, and was sufficiently convinced to take Lyell's idea a step further. If old species could slowly and naturally die out, why then should not new species be able to appear in the same way, for the same natural reasons that had eradicated their predecessors? If dying out did not require a catastrophe, why then should coming into being require creation?

Darwin continued to work on the question after his return home. 1838 was a severe year of depression—400,000 unemployed emigrated from Great Britain. That solved some of their home country's problems, but in the countries in which the emigrants arrived, they became the exterminating angels of death to the native peoples. Darwin noted that when two human races meet, they behave like two animal species—they fight, they eat each other, they infect each other. "The stronger are always extirpating the weaker"—and in his opinion "the British were beating the lot."

Darwin's theories fitted in with the social situation all round him. That was what made it so convincing when it was published in *The Origin of Species* (1859). Publication was delayed so long primarily because Darwin was frightened by his own ideas. He realized how they could be misused. He had stomach pains the moment he thought about his evolutionary theories, often vomiting for weeks.

That is not all that strange. If the inventors of the atom bomb had been afflicted with inexplicable vomiting, that would really have been rather healthy. That such a sensitive and kindly person as Darwin, who almost killed his wife with chloroform so that she should not suffer when giving birth—vomited as soon as he thought about his theory, is perhaps something that requires no further explanation.

Many of Darwin's worst apprehensions were realized. The discussions on his theory were given just those political and religious overtones he had feared. Darwin himself had avoided applying his theory to humankind. But his readers did so immediately. His theory was soon misused to legitimize inhuman competition, racism, and the extermination of other races.

Unfortunately, Darwin also allowed himself to move in that direction. In his next major work, *The Descent of Man* (1871), in chapters 5 and 6 Darwin makes the extermination of native peoples a natural element in the process of evolution. Animal species had always exterminated each other, so had savages; and now when there are civilized people, the savages will be completely exterminated: "When civilised nations come into contact with barbarians the struggle is short, except where a deadly climate gives its aid to the native race."

And not even then can the native people feel safe: "At some future period, not very distant as measured by centuries, the civilised races of man will almost certainly exterminate and replace throughout the world the savage races."

Darwin himself had seen it happen—in Argentina, in Tasmania, and in Australia—and had reacted very sharply to what he had seen. But incorporated in his evolutionary theories, the extermination of native people no longer stood out as an inhuman crime, but as the inescapable result of natural processes and the necessary prerequisite for future progress.

What Langfield Ward produced against Darwinism and the spirit of the age was not very much. He had nothing but his sense of morality. He said: It is not right to eradicate other peoples.

Ward insisted that the conquest of foreign territories brought with it certain moral obligations, and that it was the government's task to make sure these obligations were observed. "We are charged with the protection, and with the civilization of those over whom we claim dominion."

Ward asks: What is it that happens when this responsibility is ignored so that whole human races are exterminated? Infectious diseases are the usual reason, and altered ways of living, the sale of alcohol, and competition with the technically superior colonizers have also contributed to the destruction of native peoples.

But the greatest extermination factor is a special form of warfare that also involves killing women and children. That is the most effective way of stopping the defeated from ever retrieving their previous position. Extermination of that kind, the very opposite of the civilized rules of warfare, have often marked the Indian wars of this century, Ward says.

Between civilized nations, it is agreed that private property shall be respected by those who invade a country. But when it comes to native people, villages are allowed to be burned down, crops destroyed, and everything of value taken away.

However strong a tribe is, it can do nothing but react when foreigners come and take over the land that has belonged to them since time immemorial. They take to arms, and once the war has started, it does not stop until the natives have been driven out or annihilated.

Responsibility for the natives cannot be given to those who have everything to gain from expansion. Therefore, in every colony there should be a special official whose task it is to speak for the natives. (In the Spanish Empire, he was called "The Protector of the Indians.") He is to take measures against attacks on the natives and ensure that first the colonists and eventually also the natives are vaccinated against infectious diseases.

With the aid of this reform, the future, Ward hopes, will be somewhat brighter. "We may at any rate trust that the terrible crimes which deface the record of some of our earlier colonizations will not be repeated, and that the frauds by which territory was acquired will never again be perpetrated."

Ward's pious hopes were soon to come to nothing during "the scramble for Africa." In 1874, some of the darkest chapters of European expansion still lay in the future.

The voice of humanity was weak, no more than a feeble squeak. If you were humane like Ward, then you attempted to arouse compassion for the victims and prayed for mercy on their behalf. But hardly anyone questioned any longer the fundamental presumption of racism, that it was the right of whites to rule and the duty of the coloreds to submit.

Ward did ask the question: Now that we know that European colonization leads to the native population being reduced and sometimes even completely obliterated, when we know that it brings misery and death to many members of the human race, have we then the right to continue?

But he accepted the usual answer to the question, namely that the rapid increase in population in Europe made expansion necessary for its future survival. It was not enough to improve European agriculture. Some of the population must also leave the country and seek a living in the colonies. Was it wrong to settle on land already occupied? No, for many fertile areas were used only for hunting and produced no more than a small fraction of what they were capable of.

So the Europeans were considered to have the right to take over land in the colonies, partly because Europe was overpopulated and partly because Europeans could make the land produce more than the natives could. But the Asians were able to invoke both these arguments to a far greater degree. China was more overpopulated than Europe, and Chinese agriculture was far more intensive than European. So, according to this reasoning, China had a greater right to expansion in America and Australia than Europe had.

The fact was that Europe was taking over an ever greater share of the globe. The intellectual and moral reasons invoked did not hold water. Only racism could defend what Europe did and intended to continue doing. So racism flourished.

And in his opposition to genocide, Langfield Ward stood out as an eccentric remnant of a prescientific morality, which progress had long since left behind.

13

"Anti-Semitism, the monster of national emotion"

Theodor Mommsen, 1880

THREE TIMES, THE German Jews were emancipated and gained citizens' rights. Each time, the ancient, originally religiously-motivated hatred of Jews reappeared in a new guise.

The first time, in 1812, it was Napoleon who pulled down the ghetto walls. A few years later, after Napoleon was defeated, German nationalism turned with rage on the Jews, who had gained advantage from the French occupation. The Jews were accused of being nationally unreliable.

The second time, the 1848 liberal revolution emancipated the Jews. That triggered another wave of hatred of the Jews peaking when the revolution was defeated in 1849. This time the Jews were accused of being socially unreliable and adherents of extreme doctrines such as democracy and socialism.

The third time, the Jews were emancipated with the union of Germany in 1870. By the end of the 1870s, the reaction set in. This time it was not just the Jews' religion, nationality and political opinions that were wrong, but their actual hereditary disposition. The Jews were said to be racially inferior to other Germans.

Those making this statement were indeed not able to agree on whether the Jews constituted one, two, three, or more races, or exactly in which way their hereditary disposition could be distinguished from that of other whites. But by making use of the concept of race, they appeared to have scientific support for their hatred—just as white Americans previously had sought scientific support for their hatred of Native Americans, African Americans, and Chinese.

Can the inspiration have come from America?

The word "emancipation" was used in the mid-1800s to describe both the liberation of blacks from slavery in the United States and the liberation of the Jews from the ghettos of Europe. Reading early anti-Semitic works such as the political economist Eugen Dühring's *Die Judenfrage als Racen-, Sitten- und Culturfrage* (1881), one is struck by the similarity in reactions and arguments among the opponents of emancipation on both sides of the Atlantic.

Both Jews and blacks were considered racially unfit for liberty, "zur Freiheit unfähig." For the opponents of emancipation, both Jews and blacks constituted such an impending threat that the strongest countermeasures were necessary. "It would be a complete misunderstanding of the concept of humanity," wrote Dühring, "if you hesitated, even for a moment, to direct the fight against the Jews towards permanently rendering them harmless *dauernde Unschädlichmachung*." Similar statements on black people were made in the United States both before and after the Civil War.

In at least one case, it is possible to establish a direct American influence.

One of the first racial anti-Semites, Wilhelm Marr, began his public career as an advocate for Jewish emancipation. He was also an atheist and a radical democrat. After the 1848 revolution, he emigrated, as did many other defeated revolutionaries, to America.

In New York, he discovers to his indignation that here, in the birthplace of freedom, black people are not allowed to ride in the same tram as whites. In protest, he boards the blacks' tram and lands between two fat black men who smell so foul, he gets off the tram at the very next stop, professing considerably greater understanding of segregated trams.

Marr's book *Reise nach Centralamerika* (1863) contains several racist anecdotes of this kind. It describes a European democrat's schooling in American racial prejudices and faith in white supremacy. After seven years in Nicaragua and Costa Rica, when Marr returns to Europe, it is as a fully fledged racist: "The fact that we whites are better than the blacks and that a black never achieves the cultural level of a white, Nicaragua has engraved in Gothic script on my mind."

Back in Hamburg, Marr was excluded from the democratic movement for defending black slavery and attacking the Jews. He failed in business, divorced his rich Jewish wife, lost his second Jewish wife in childbirth, and his third to a fellow anti-Semite. In the 1870s, he was struggling on as a freelance journalist in Berlin, a bitter rejected man who blamed the failure of his life on the Jews.

The Jews had already won, he wrote in *Der Sieg des Judenthums über das Germanenthum* (1879). Marr writes, he says in the foreword, from a natural sciences standpoint and explains that the "Jewish question," like the "Negro question," is a "question of race." He puts it most clearly in an article at the same time: "The Jew is a white Negro."

This new garment for the old Jew hatred turned out to be

profitable—Marr's book became a best-seller that was published in twelve editions and William Marr wrote himself into history as "the father of modern anti-Semitism".

The timing was well chosen. Many Germans blamed the Jews for the wave of speculation that had led to the 1873 stock exchange crash and for the long depression that followed. In actual fact, the depression was international and everywhere provoked persecution of whatever minority was nearest to hand: on the U.S. West Coast, it was the Chinese; on the East Coast, the blacks, and in Europe, the Jews.

Even in comparatively tolerant England, hostility to the Jews increased during the 1870s. But the Jewish people also had influential defenders—George Eliot dedicated her last two books, *Daniel Deronda* (1876) and *Impressions of Theophratus Such* (1879), to the struggle against increasing anti-Jewish prejudice.

In Germany, these prejudices became particularly strong. The new German union was still fragile and threatened with antagonisms between the previous small German states, as well as between different religions, regions, and social classes. It was tempting to exploit anti-Jewish feelings in an attempt to bridge inner tensions and unite the nation.

In November 1879, the conservative nationalist, Heinrich von Treitschke, one of Germany's most well-known social scientists, wrote a column on the anti-Jewish movements that had just begun to organize. His attitude to them was, to say the least, ambiguous and came to function as legitimation for anti-Semitism.

Treitschke distanced himself from violent actions, but at the same time defended "the brutal and fierce but natural reaction of the people's Germanic spirit to an alien element which has come to occupy far too great a place in our lives." The Jews ought not to be deprived of their citizen's rights, he said, but at the same time he saw popular hostility to the Jews as an expression of the healthy instinct of the masses. It could also be found in the very best educated, who agreed that "the Jews are our misfortune."

The misfortune, according to Treitschke, was rapidly growing. "From the limitless Polish cradle, year after year, across our eastern border pours a stream of industrious, trouser-selling youths whose children and grandchildren will soon control Germany's stock exchanges and newspapers. The more this immigration increases, the more serious will become the question of how this alien race can be integrated with ours."

A Jewish statistician, S. Neuman, was promptly able to show that Treitschke's worries over Jewish mass immigration were factually unfounded. Of the 562,000 Jews living in Germany, only 15,000, or three percent were born abroad. As part of the German people, these 15,000 Jewish immigrants were a drop in the ocean.

But objections of that kind did not affect Treitschke's enormous prestige. A greater authority than himself would have to speak up. There was essentially only one: his professorial colleague, Theodor Mommsen, specialist in Roman history, and ever since the 1848 revolution, known for his liberal and democratic standpoints.

The counterattack came in November 1880, when seventy-three leaders in science, politics, and commerce made public a protest against the anti-Jewish agitation. At the same time,

Mommsen in his essay *Auch ein Wort über unser Judenthum* put Treitschke up against the wall by asking him what it really meant when he "demanded of our Jewish citizens that they should become Germans."

"They already are," wrote Mommsen. "Just as good as he and I are."

They are indeed not of Germanic origin, Mommsen went on. But the French anthropologist, Armand de Quatrefages, has shown that the same applies to large parts of the remaining German population. The Prussians, for instance, consist to a great extent of "decayed Slavs" and other groups whom the anti-Semites regard as "human scum."

Indeed there are differences between Jews and Teutons, but such differences are also found between other Germans of different origins, different religions, and from different parts of the country. Today, the drive is against Jews. Tomorrow it may apply to Berliners. By warring against the Jews, we are treading a dangerous path that does not lead to unity but, on the contrary, may reawaken old disputes between north and south, east and west.

Treitschke had certainly not wanted that. But the question is: What had he wanted? When he treats the Jews as second-class citizens, he is inviting mobs of all classes to leap on defenseless prey. That is to preach civil war.

The witch hunt of today, Mommsen hoped, will pass and tolerance return—not just religious tolerance toward the synagogue, but, even more important, respect for the Jewish way of life.

It is, of course, our duty to protect the civil rights of the Jews. What we cannot protect them against is the feeling of alienation, which anti-Semitism — "the monster of national emotion"—inescapably arouses in them. That entails a danger to both parties, for the very possibility of a civil war of the majority against a minority is a national misfortune, Mommsen writes.

Through "the Berlin battle over anti-Semitism," as this debate was called, the new word "anti-Semitism" appeared for the first time. But the battle was not really about anti-Semitism in the sense that Wilhelm Marr, Eugen Dühring and the other leading anti-Semites had meant. Their hostility to the Jews was biologically motivated and even the complete abandonment of the Jewish identity that Trietschke demanded would, according to them, only make the Jews even more dangerous.

The difference was decisive. The old demands on the Jews—that they should abandon their religion, their loyalty to the Jewish people, their political opinions, or their capitalist behaviour—were obviously unreasonable, but nevertheless theoretically possible to fulfill. But if it were the Jewish people's race with which something was wrong, there was nothing the Jews themselves or anyone else could do about it. The anti-Semites had constructed the "problem" in such a way that it could not be solved except by extermination.

At the time, Eugen Dühring was still content to issue veiled threats. He talked about the Jews as "an inner Carthage" —Carthage was famous for having been completely wiped out by the Romans.

When the German linguist Paul de Lagarde attacked the "weaklings who are too cowardly to stamp out the Jewish vermin," according to his own statements, he "only" wanted to achieve that the Jews should be deprived of their money and their power. But his images spoke another language. "One does not negotiate with trichinae and bacteria. One does not try to educate them; they are destroyed as quickly and thoroughly as possible."

Dühring also sharpened his tone of voice as each new edition came out. "The world must completely settle the bill with the Hebrew people," he wrote shortly before his death in 1921. It was the Nordic man's duty to "exterminate the parasitic races, just as one exterminates poisonous snakes and savage predators."

Was this still just images? In a 1944 German military instruction book, the metaphors, in all events, have been turned into terrible reality:

> Even today there are still among our people those who within themselves are not absolutely convinced when we are talking about the extermination of Jews in our living space.
>
> The Jew wants to force us into a life of slavery, to be able to live as a parasite on us and exploit us.
>
> Talk of compassion and love of your neighbour does not belong in a struggle of that kind. Who believes that a parasite, a louse for instance, can improve and change itself? Who believes he can come to an agreement with the parasite? We face the choice between being eaten by the parasite or destroying him. The Jew must be annihilated everywhere we come across him. With that we do not commit any crime against life, but are obeying its laws, which demand struggle against everything that is the enemy of healthy life. That is how our struggle serves the preservation of life.

Theodor Mommsen would never in his wildest dreams have been able to imagine anything of that kind. When he received the 1903 Nobel Prize for Literature just before he died, German anti-Semitism appeared to have been overcome. During the 1890s, the anti-Semites had gained fewer and fewer votes in elections, their organizations were warring with each other and dissolving, their newspapers going bankrupt; and the leading anti-Semites had died, emigrated, or fallen into poverty and insignificance.

The battle appeared to be won. And yet it had hardly begun.

14

A Century of Dishonor

Helen Hunt, 1881

DARWIN BELIEVED THAT the United States had become a great nation through natural selection: the most energetic and courageous had emigrated to the New World, he wrote in *The Descent of Man* (1871).

A view of that kind was naturally not unwelcome in America. The political economist, Francis Amsa Walker, at the Massachusetts Institute of Technology, was convinced that the successes of the United States were due to the superiority of the race. On the whole, the immigrants were of the major Germanic races and constituted a positive selection within them:

> The possibilities of improvement which reside in breeding from higher, stronger, more alert and aggressive individuals of a species are well recognized in the case of domestic animals; but there have been few opportunities for obtaining a measure of the effect that could be produced upon the human race, by excluding from the propagation the weak, the vicious, the cowardly, the effeminate, persons of

dwarfed stature, of tainted blood, or of imperfect organization.

But Walker considered America one of those rare opportunities. The inhabitants of the United States constituted a selection representing mental power, intellectual curiosity, enterprise, and self-confidence.

Settler life had honed this biological inheritance to perfection. Industry also looked as if it would be a good schooling. There the pace of work was regulated entirely by technology, which had a character-forming effect on the workers.

Langfield Ward had suggested that a special official be appointed to protect the natives in every British colony. In the United States, there already was such an official. In the early 1870s, Walker was appointed as Commissioner for Indian Affairs. In his first annual report in 1872, he produced a plan for the rehabilitation of the Indian.

Walker suggested that the reserves for the Indians should be what the factory was for the white worker: a reformatory. The reserves would not only contain the Indians but also train them and improve them. Most of all, it was a matter of putting them to hard work.

The Indians were not to be allowed to leave the reserves without special permission. Only in that way could they learn to control their "strong animal appetites." Walker himself was grateful for the thrashings he had received as a child. That had taught him self-control. The Indian could learn the same through "a severe course of industrial instruction and exercise under restraint."

Anyone refusing to cooperate and obstructing progress had to be "relentlessly crushed." The Indians were to "yield or perish." The reserve as reformatory was the only way to "save the remnants of the Indian race from destruction."

Was there really no other way?

Helen Fiske was the best friend and playmate of the poet Emily Dickinson. Helen married a Mr. Hunt and became a housewife. But when Hunt died in a submarine experiment, she became a writer to support herself and her children. Her soulful stories and lively travel writings became popular, but would today have been totally forgotten had she not happened to go to Colorado.

That was where she met a banker and railway owner by the name of William Jackson and married for the second time. That was also where she came face to face with Indians. That was where she wrote, swiftly, breathlessly, raging with indignation, the book that made her world-famous: *A Century of Dishonor* (1881).

Helen Hunt has been called the "Indians' Harriet Beecher Stowe," but her style is quite different and much dryer than that of *Uncle Tom's Cabin*. She does not write one single person's history of suffering, but that of entire peoples; and she appeals to a sense of justice rather than to compassion. She maintains that the treatment of the Indians is contrary to international law.

This statement appears at first to be quite foolish, for the standard works of international law were written by white jurists who had long since adapted to the realities of European expansion.

The leading British authority was William Edward Hall and in his *A Treatise on International Law* (first edition 1880, last 1924), Chapter 2 deals with colonial acquisition of land and land disputes. What is discussed is exclusively conflicts between "civilized" states and their claim to other people's territory. The idea that the other indigenous peoples should be allowed some rights or opinions is never even considered.

The leading French authority was Arthur Girault and his *Principes de colonisation et de législation coloniale* (first edition 1894, last 1923). He has exactly the same attitude as Hall, but expresses himself more bluntly: The question of the rights of colonization, he says, "is whether Europeans should have to resign themselves to the miseries of overpopulation for a few thousand natives to be able to continue to eat each other."

Then he adds: "The gradual eradication of the lower races by the civilised races, or if another choice of words is preferred, the annihilation by the strong of the weak, is the actual prerequisite for progress."

The leading German authority, Rudolf von Ihering, said in the introduction to his *Geist des römischen Rechts* (first edition 1852):

> History has taught peoples that no absolute right to ownership exists. The seeming wrong the Anglo-Saxon race is committing against the natives in America is a right from the point of view of universal history; and the European peoples are no less within their rights when they open the rivers and harbours of China and Japan by force and make their peoples partake in trade. For trading is both a right and a duty. To refuse to fulfil this duty [the duty to trade in opium] is to revolt against nature's order and the decree of history.

Helen Hunt would not have stood a chance if she had questioned these authorities. She was far too clever even to attempt it. She agreed with them, all of them, and reserved judgment only on one single little point: She considered that agreements entered into should be adhered to.

It was a point that all the judicial authorities adhered to strictly in all other contexts. The faith in agreements entered into maintains individual states as well as international society, says Hugo Grotius, "the father of international law" (1583–1645). Remove that faith, Aristotle says, and all human communion collapses.

Naturally, such a fundamental principle must also apply to dealings between civilized states and the indigenous peoples of North America, Helen Hunt maintained.

Then she quite simply related the history of the treaties, tribe by tribe, people by people. The history of the Cherokees is an example.

The English were the first to arrive, in 1733, on Cherokee land, and they would never have survived the winter without the peace and aid treaty they agreed to with the Native Americans.

For two decades, the small community struggled against difficulties and adversities. Again and again, they were close to being conquered by the French or the Spaniards, but were saved by their allies, the Cherokees.

In 1752, the colony was taken over by the English Crown, which at once broke the treaty. The betrayals and massacres by the whites led to a war that lasted for ten years.

At the peace treaty of 1763, the Cherokees were forced to hand over a large area of land to the king of England. The Indians kept their side of the treaty even when the American War of Independence broke out—and thus found themselves on the losing side. The atrocities committed by both sides became for white Americans evidence of the innate inhumanity of the Indians.

The U.S. government took up diplomatic relations with the Cherokee people through the Hopewell Treaty of 1785. This is what the representative of the United States said:

> Congress is now the sovereign of all our country which we now point out to you on the map. They want none of your lands, nor anything else which belongs to you; and as an earnest of their regard for you, we propose to enter into articles of a treaty perfectly equal and conformable to what we now tell you.

The chieftains demanded that the white men who had trespassed on areas, which according to the old treaties belonged to the Cherokees, were to be evicted, but finally agreed to receive payment for their lost lands. New boundaries were staked out and a general feeling of trust and goodwill prevailed.

Four years later, the U.S. Secretary of War wrote in a report that the Hopewell Treaty had been entirely disregarded by the white population in the area. Many unprovoked outrages had been committed against the Cherokees, leading to fighting that had drastically reduced the number of Cherokees.

In 1791, the Indians were forced to give up more land at the Treaty of Holston. In 1794, it became necessary to draw up a new treaty to confirm the validity of the Treaty of Holston.

In 1801, the United States once again applied to purchase land the white settlers had seized in violation of the treaty.

This time the Cherokees refused; but after four years of negotiations, they were finally forced to hand over several large areas of land in exchange for promises that they should retain the remainder forever.

In 1816, the time came again. The Cherokees lost all their land in South Carolina. In 1822, the Cherokees wrote to the Senate requesting protection according to the treaty. The state of Georgia called the paper "insults from the polluted lips of outcasts and vagabonds" and threatened civil war if the government opposed the occupation of the Indians' land.

By this time, every Cherokee family had a small farm and many of them were occupied carding and spinning cotton. Every district had a courthouse, judge, and police. A national council was the nation's supreme authority. There was a school in every village and often a church as well.

In December 1829, Georgia passed a law abolishing the civil rights of the Cherokees. The U.S. government confirmed the state's right to take over the Indians' lands. Georgia declared a state of emergency and parceled out the Indians' land among the whites. Appeal after appeal to the Senate and the president to uphold the treaty were met with exhortations to move westwards. Even in the Supreme Court, the majority voted against the Cherokees, deciding that they were not "a foreign nation" in the true sense of the term and so could not bring suit against the United States.

By the terms of a new treaty in 1835, the Indians gave up all their territory and were given five million dollars, seven million acres west of the Mississipi, "and free and unmolested use of all the country west of the western boundary of said seven million of acres, as far west as the sovereignty of the United States and their rights of soil extend."

The treaty also states that the land handed over to the Indians "shall in no future time, without their consent, be included within the territorial limits or jurisdiction of any State or Territory."

A great many Cherokees were against the treaty. They were removed by military force. For many years afterward, the question of whether the removal had been inevitable was still being discussed. But gradually life began to return. In 1851, the Cherokees had twenty-two schools, a teetotal society of three thousand members with a branch in every district, twelve churches, eight courts, and a national council elected every four years.

During the American Civil War, the Indians once again found themselves on the losing side. In 1865, they had to buy their peace by giving up large areas of land.

The rest was to be theirs forever. In 1870, the Department of the Interior assured them that the treaty with the Cherokees was an expression of the United States' anxious desire to "secure to the Cherokee nation of Indians a permanent home, and which shall, under the most solemn guarantee of the United States, be and remain theirs forever."

But as soon as six years later, the same department under the influence of the Indian Commissioner Francis A. Walker had realized the matter was more complicated than that. Should a large part of the land really be allowed to lie uncultivated?

Naturally, treaties should not be broken, nor should injustices be done to the Indians. But "there is a very general and growing opinion that observance of the strict letter of treaties with Indians is in many cases at variance with their own best interests and with sound public policy."

That is where we stand now, Helen Hunt wrote in 1881.

What to do? One thing only. We must stop—stop robbing, stop cheating, stop breaking our promises. We must admit that the Indians also have a right to their property and a right to "life, liberty and the pursuit of happiness."

What happened?

Helen Hunt's book became a best-seller that shook America's conscience.

It also became a much-hated book. Theodore Roosevelt, the future president, was disgusted by constantly seeing it quoted by "maudlin fanatics," and added: "I don't go so far as to think that the only good Indians are the dead Indians, but I believe nine out of every ten are, and I shouldn't inquire too closely into the case of the tenth."

Helen Hunt fought against that attitude in vain. Her book could not stop the notorious Daws Act of 1887, which parcelled out parts of the reserve lands into small lots to individual Indians. The rest was sold to the whites and the money put in a foundation to finance "educating and civilising" the Indians according to a model reminiscent of the Walker Plan's reformatories.

That law was valid until 1934. By then, sixty percent of the land owned by the Indians in 1887 had passed into white ownership—all for their own good.

15

The Silent South

George Cable, 1885

THE WORD "LYNCHING" acquired its modern meaning—mob killing, murder committed by an excited crowd—after the American Civil War (1861–65).

The Northern states punished the rebellion of the South (that is how the South saw it) by abolishing slavery and giving the black people of the Southern states citizen's rights. When the last federal troops left the South in 1877, the white minority gradually began using violence and threats to regain power.

The number of lynchings increased dramatically until 1892, when 69 whites and 162 blacks were murdered by screaming mobs. While violence against the Chinese in California or against Jews in Russia came in waves with intervening calmer periods, the number of lynchings in the American South remained constant at over a hundred a year until 1904.

Why were black people murdered? The standard answer was because they had raped white women. But a study of 3,811 blacks lynched between 1889 and 1941 shows that in only seventeen percent of cases had the crowd alleged that there had been any attempt to commit rape. Blacks were lynched for quite different reasons—because they tried to register as voters, for trade union activities, and most of all for being "uppity," that is, a lack of servility toward the whites.

The lynched men were sometimes fatally beaten, sometimes hanged, sometimes burned to death on bonfires. They were quite often killed by drawn-out torture in everyone's view. The intention was to make examples of them. The lynchings were a way of restoring through terror the domination of the white minority. When this domination had found expression in new segregation laws which were upheld by the judiciary, the number of lynchings fell to "only" just under fifty a year during the 1904–15 period.

In 1875, a threatening crowd of white men assembled one day outside a girls' school in New Orleans, calling out the black girls one by one—only the white girls were allowed to stay in school. The following day, the local newspaper published a letter by "a Southern White Man" protesting against the mob's attack on a school that had hitherto functioned well for both blacks and whites.

In the days of slavery, no one had cared if white and black children played together or even whether a white child was fed at a black breast, he wrote. Why had it become more dangerous now? Why should blacks not be accepted as teachers if they were better or equally well-qualified as whites? And where would those who had recommended two separate but equal school systems find the money for the increased costs?

Education for the black people, whose ignorance today lies like a nightmare over the South, is the best investment in the future. The writer ended his letter, "It is in every citizen's interest to have the masses educated."

The letter was published together with an equally long editorial reply stating that "African proclivities are towards savagery and cannibalism.

"The only condition under which the two races can coexist peacefully is that in which the superior race shall control and the inferior race shall obey. . . . For our part we hope never to see the white boys and girls of America forgetful of the fact that negroes are their inferiors."

With that, the newspaper considered the matter closed.

George Cable, who had sent the letter, was born in 1844 into a slave-owning family in New Orleans. At fourteen, as the eldest son, he took over his deceased father's job and the responsibility of breadwinner. At nineteen he took part in the Civil War, and at twenty-six he began writing for an hour every morning before he went to his job as a bookkeeper. At thirty-five he published his first book of fiction, and at thirty-eight was proclaimed the greatest writer in the South and received an honorary doctorate from Mississippi University.

At forty, he put all this at stake with his book *The Silent South* (1885)—a fiery appeal to the whites not to stay silent while the racists took power.

Cable first attacked the failings of white "justice." He studied the reports on the treatment of offenders and found that blacks regularly received more than twice as long sentences as whites did for the same crime. Black people were punished for petty theft with twelve, fifteen, twenty, even in one case forty years hard labor—in camps that killed inmates within five years on an average.

The thinking behind this was that the prisons should be

made "self-supporting." But why? Schools, courts, and legislative assemblies were not self-supporting. Why should prisons be?

The features of the system varied in different regions. Sometimes the prisoners were hired out in gangs of a few hundred to private firms or public works. In some cases, the actual prison was leased out, together with the prisoners, sometimes for a year, sometimes five, occasionally twenty years.

The fundamental thinking was that the state owned the prisoner's person and had the opportunity to earn money from its property. The most profitable treatment of offenders was therefore considered the best, regardless of any moral consequences or fatal outcome for the prisoners.

In Tennessee, the auditors wrote: "Rentals have been promptly paid, and the prisoners worked in accordance with law and [are] most humanely treated . . . To our minds there can be no valid objection raised to the Lease System, under proper restrictions, especially if as well conducted as for the past few years."

That year, the state had 1,336 prisoners, of whom half were scattered in various camps, most of them at coal mines. A column in a record book of the period listed the cause of death: "Found dead. Killed. Drowned. Not given. Blank. Blank. Blank. Killed. Blank. Blank. Killed. Killed. Blank. Blank. Blank. Killed. Blank. Blank." The reports stated that only men in good health were sent to the mines. It was quite usual that injured or sick men were returned to prison and replaced by others. And yet mortality was frightfully high.

In North Carolina, camp mortality was eight times higher than in Sing-Sing. Of 776 men building a railway, 178 died during the year. For 158 of them, there was no information on the cause of death.

The registers of prisoners showed that no prisoner had managed to stay alive for more than ten years in Georgia's penal institutions. But of the state's 1,200 prisoners, 538 were sentenced to ten years or more, often for petty theft. In other words, for simple theft, with no break-in or violence, the majority of the prisoners in this American gulag had been condemned to death through hard labor.

The system invited abuse. White men more or less had a monopoly on juries. The general public wanted mines, roads and railways built, but no one wanted to pay for them. There was a tremendous temptation to give blacks extravagant sentences, and sell their labor to the highest bidder who would use them in the construction of public works.

Ultimately it was a question of white supremacy. "Everyone of us grew up in the idea that he had, by birth and race, certain broad powers of police over any and every person of color," Cable says. Such ideas bind us together. For more than a hundred years it is on them we have built our identity and self-respect.

"I myself am the son and grandson of slave-owners," Cable goes on. They had their faults; posterity will discover ours. The important thing is that we speak, and speak frankly and fearlessly about these faults, in order to find out the real needs of our society. The silence of the South must be broken.

Our forefathers did not always act justly, but for their own peace of mind, they had to believe that they had done so. So they talked much of "the negro's contentment with the servile condition for which nature has designed him." For the former owners of the emancipated slaves, the main question was how to uphold the unfounded idea that all whites were superior to blacks and the equally unfounded idea that all blacks were the same and constituted an alien, dangerous class suited only for physical labor.

The courts of the South had become an instrument to perpetuate these prejudices and keep blacks down. But by holding the Negro down, Cable believed, we sink ourselves. "It is the first premise of American principles that whatever elevates the lower stratum of the people lifts all the rest, and whatever holds it down holds all down."

Cable's appeal to the Southern whites was fruitless. After all, it was 1885 and in Berlin the major powers were assembled to divide Africa among themselves. The entire grand power structure was inconsistent with blacks having the vote. It was based on the same conviction of the superiority of the white race that lay behind white supremacy in the Southern states.

In America, the imperial era did not begin until 1898, when the United States defeated Spain and took over previously Spanish colonies with eight million colored inhabitants, "a varied assortment of inferior races, which of course could not be allowed to vote," to quote *The Nation*.

"At the very time that imperialism was sweeping the country, the doctrine of racism reached a crest of acceptability and popularity among respectable scholarly and intellectual circles," says Vann Woodward (1966), a leading American scholar in this field.

But the foundations had been laid, he goes on, during the long-lasting depression in the South in the 1880s and 1890s. Frustrated whites sought outlets for their aggressions in violence against the scapegoats, blacks. The press wallowed in news reports of black crime, arrogance, and impertinence. Signals came from all directions indicating that it was acceptable to hate.

But the decisive condition for the victory of extreme racism in the South, according to Woodward, was that the opposition offered insufficient resistance. Fear, hatred, and fanaticism had long existed in varying degrees of intensity. What allowed racists to prevail was that the counterforces were weakened. Liberals in the North, conservatives and radicals in the South—they all lost their self-confidence and fell silent.

One of the few who really did resist was George Cable. He staked everything and lost. Now, afterward, the documents show that he had many secret sympathizers among the whites of the South. But when the tide went against Cable, they did not dare do anything but remain silent.

The racist reaction against Cable's book was powerful. He was called a traitor who had sold the South for success in the North. "Not a few of us have been heartily disgusted with the cringing, crawling, dirt-eating spirit shown by Mr. Cable and some of his satellites."

The newspaper in New Orleans for which he used to write led the attack. Cable's ideas would lead to social chaos and racial war, it said. His aim was "to degrade, lower in the public opinion the reputation of the population of Louisiana, Creole or not, to put it socially, civilly and politically below the black race, which he considers superior to ours and destined to Africanize the entire South," etc.

The discussion raged for eight years without any real dialogue being possible. Disgraced and detested, Cable was forced to move to the North. He never regained his creativity. At his death in 1925, white supremacy in the South was still unbroken.

16

White Natives of Europe

William D. Babington, 1895

> I am haunted by the human chimpanzees I saw along that hundred miles of horrible country. I don't believe they are our fault. I believe there are not only many more of them than of old, but they are happier, better, more comfortably fed and lodged under our rule than they ever were. But to see white chimpanzees is dreadful; if they were black, one would not feel it so much, but their skins, except where tanned by exposure, are as white as ours.

The Irish were Europe's white natives. They frightened the famous writer and historian Charles Kingsley, traveling in Ireland in 1860, because the color of their skin did not conform to his racial prejudices. In 1815, Henri Grégoire had seen nothing biologically strange about the Irish situation; he saw the English colonial oppression and protested against it. As a Catholic, he demanded civil rights for Catholics as well as for Protestants. On his journey to Ireland in 1835, Tocqueville was equally aware that the wretchedness of the Irish had political and economic causes.

But in the latter half of the nineteenth century, biological causes were eagerly sought, rather than political and economic ones. If the Irish lived in misery and oppression, then that must be due to the fact that they were "chimpanzees," that is, biologically different from other white people.

Allegedly inborn racial characteristics became the standard explanation for all variations between different societies. How then could obvious differences between peoples and societies of the same race be explained? That was what confused Kingsley.

The solution was to invent new races and sub-races that were said to explain biologically the history and social circumstances of the group. So starting from the language families, the white race was divided up into Germanics, Slavs, Celts, Semites, and these groups into smaller and smaller subdivisions until every nation, even every province, appeared as a "race" of its own with its special "disposition" or "character."

When fundamental criticism of the basis of racism began again in the 1890s after having lain low for almost half a century, it was these so-called "national characteristics" in particular that came to the fore.

A pioneer among these critics was William D. Babington with his fragmentary, posthumously published book *Fallacies of Race Theories as Applied to National Characteristics* (1895). His criticism was developed more fully by John Mackinnon Robertson in *The Saxon and the Celt—a Study in Sociology* (1897).

Judging an individual's character correctly is a difficult task—that was Babington's starting point. Could anyone imagine it to be easier to acertain the character of a group consisting of several million people?

Where is the English national character to be studied—in the prosperous middle class or among the poor who make up the majority? How is the observer to avoid being influenced by his or her own patriotism and other preconceived notions?

The French seldom agree with the high estimate Germans have formed of "the German." Germans often have a highly unfavorable opinion of "the French." Words such as "the German" quite simply have no equivalent in reality—all we can observe is real Germans, who are all dissimilar. And yet, out of habit, we talk about "the German" as if he or she really existed, ascribing to him or her all kinds of qualities.

Babington quotes the famous Oxford historian Edward A. Freeman, who defends the belief in national characteristics in this way:

> There is in each nation, in each race, a dominant element, or rather something more than an element, something which is the true essence of the race or nation, something which sets its standard and determines its character, something which draws to itself and assimilates to itself all the other elements.

This is nothing more than the Real Essence of medieval scholastics, Babington objects. If a nation can be said to have a characteristic, then that statement must be based on something more tangible than long since refuted metaphysics.

The fact that Babington turned against Freeman in particular was no matter of chance. Freeman was one of the most respected historians of the day and his view of history was based on a racism as comprehensive as it was profound.

Naturally, he despised Jews, blacks, and Chinese; but his particular object of hatred was the Irish.

The English, according to Freeman, were really a kind of German. German was the finest anyone could be. Modern Germans were unfortunately no longer sufficiently German, and in France, German blood had almost been wasted in the original population, the Celts, as the latter had been allowed to live. The Germans, the so-called Angles and Saxons who invaded the British Isles, had fortunately set about it more thoroughly. They had as good as completely eradicated the original Celtic population and pushed the remainder into Cornwall, Wales, and Ireland—all according to Freeman.

The success of England, to put it briefly, was due to one fundamental biological and cultural fact: that the country had become purely English, that is to say German, through mass murder of the defeated Irish.

Freeman began to propound this teaching in the 1860s. It was published in huge editions of his *Old English History for Children* (1869), and in his pupil John Green's *Short History of the English People* (1874). The Freeman doctrine was particularly successful on his lecture tour of the United States in 1882. There he emphasized that the Germans, the English, and the Americans were really the same people, who had simply moved from their first home in Germany to their second home in England, and from there to their third home in the United States.

In both their second and third "homes," the original inhabitants had been thoroughly exterminated. In Freeman's use of language, the concept of "exterminate" included both those who had been killed and those who had been driven away. But the idea that what Americans had done to the

Indians was nothing but a natural continuation of what their forefathers had done to the Celts—that won approval in America.

The future president Theodore Roosevelt wrote in his book *The Winning of the West* (1889) that the migration by which the American continent had been conquered and populated must be regarded in its context with the "racial history" of the participating nations.

"The English had exterminated or assimilated the Celts of Britain, and they substantially repeated the process with the Indians of America; although of course in America there was very little, instead of very much, assimilation." When the settlers in Australia and New Zealand exterminated the natives, they were only doing their share of the work that had begun with the conquest of Britain and had culminated in the wonderful growth of the United States.

Had this growth now reached its natural limits? No, John Fiske, a leading American historian lecturing at the Royal Institution in London in 1880, did not think so.

There was still a great deal to be done. We can leave the details for the moment, Fiske said.

> It is enough to point to the general conclusion, that the work which the English race began when it colonized North America is destined to go on until every land on the earth's surface that is not already seat of an old civilization shall become English in its language, in its political habits and traditions and to a predominant extent in the blood of its people.
>
> The day is at hand when four fifths of the human race will trace its pedigree to English forefathers, as

four fifths of the white people in the United States trace their pedigree to-day.

The original genocide the Saxons once committed at the dawn of history when they exterminated the forefathers of the Irish has in Fiske's vision of history spread all over the globe and populated almost the entire world with the English.

Babington criticized the Freeman doctrine primarily for its enormous overestimation of the Germans. The old Germanics were simply savages living in dirty hovels, pastoral people who detested work and loved fighting. They drank, gambled, and quarrelled as savages are apt to do.

To put it briefly, they were just as lazy, bibulous, and unruly as the Celts were accused of being. They simply demonstrated the qualities we can expect to find in all peoples on an equivalent level of development. But neither in the Germanics nor the Celts have these characteristsics turned out to be inevitable elements in their "racial character," Babington adds.

To the extent that there are differences between the English and the Irish, they are due to factors other than race. Why should it be presumed that the original Celtic inhabitants of the British Isles were exterminated? The most competent anthropologists maintain the contrary, that both Celts and Saxons were integral elements of the new nation.

The majority of the original population remained and then a new injection of alien blood came via the Norman conquest and widespread immigration, not least from Ireland. The result has become a mixed race with a great many different elements.

In the corresponding way, the Irish people are of mixed ancestry. This truth is denied both by Irish patriots, who honor the Celtic race, and by those who defend English rule on the score that the Celts by nature are incapable of ruling themselves.

The truth is that since the sixteenth century English policies have sought the eradication of the Irish, replacing them with English colonizers and landowners. Complete eradication was never achieved in Ireland, and actually both races became almost completely mixed.

How then can the differences between the Irish and the English be explained? By environment, legislation, political history, and religion. Those are the determining factors; and there is no reason to invent any fairy tales about "Celtic blood" or, for that matter, "Anglo-Saxon blood."

"It is therefore only a foolish vanity which leads any one nation to fancy that it possesses inborn gifts different from those of others, such as enable it by these alone to maintain a permanent intellectual superiority," Babington concludes.

17

How Perilous Is the Yellow Peril?

Jacques Novicow, 1897

EVERY AGE HAS its anguish. In 1900, at the turn of the century, Europe was at the height of its powers, and at the same time was obsessed by the fear of losing those powers.

The German historian Heinz Gollwitzer has studied one of the many nightmares of the people of the late 1800s; It was called the Yellow Peril.

The expression became popular in France in connection with the Sino-Japanese War in 1894, then spread rapidly to other countries to culminate when the Japanese defeated Russia in 1905. Then the slogan became rarer but never entirely died out.

One of the first to warn against the Yellow Peril was the Oxford historian Charles H. Pearson. In 1892, when he returned to England after a period in Australia, he was appalled—free enterprise seemed to him to have been abandoned in favor of the destructive principles of the welfare state, leading to the demise of the family, failing business morale, and a weakening of artistic creativity.

Ruined by its welfare policies, Britain was now faced

with the threat of the Far East becoming industrialized. As the black and yellow people increased in numbers faster than the whites, the situation seemed hopeless in the long term. The Chinese would take the lead and command the colored peoples in their striving for freedom from European domination.

The day is not far off, Pearson predicted with a shudder, when the Chinese and the Latin Americans (yes, perhaps even the Africans) will sit with equal rights at the negotiation table as members of international society.

Even gloomier was the American historian Brooks Adams. In *America's Economic Supremacy* (1900), he believed that he belonged to a decrepit race no longer capable of upholding the conditions for a civilized society, and which was also severely threatened by other continents. "Should Asia industrialise and achieve independence, the result would be the immediate downfall of the United States and the rest of the civilised world."

Experts on the Far East tried to calm Pearson and Adams with the fact that neither China nor Japan had hitherto constituted any real threat. On the contrary, China was about to be divided up among the major powers—the only problem for Britain and the United States was how to acquire the most luscious bits. East Asia should be regarded as a major, almost limitless opportunity for commercial expansion.

In France, the feeling of national decay was particularly widespread. Beyond the turn of the century lay the chasm of a yellow Europe. The Chinese and Japanese would take over, just as the barbarians had taken over the Roman Empire. But at least they had been barbarians of the same race as the Romans. Only the white race had supported a civilization that continued to develop at a rapidly increasing pace. A yellow Europe would entail a new Dark Ages, as the voices of doom put it.

The Russo-French sociologist Jacques Novicow (1849–1912), pacifist, feminist, and antiracist, analyzed this fear of the Yellow Peril in his book, *L'Avenir de la race blanche* (*The Future of the White Race*) (1897).

These gloomy predictions were based on the presumption that civilization depends on race. But what really is race? Novicow asked. Some count 150 races, others only five. For some, it is the shape of the cranium that defines the race, for others the color of skin, and for yet others the hair. The confusion is total.

Even if we admitted a certain number of races with clearly defined separate characteristics at a certain point in time, as soon as we turned our backs, they would mix with each other so that once again there would be hopeless confusion.

Everyone realizes that civilization has no direct connection with shape of skull or color of skin. If any connection exists at all, it must be indirect. Physiological characteristics must be connected with mental abilities to be able to cause a new Dark Ages.

But hitherto no evidence whatsoever exists of any such connection. Everything has been investigated—the weight of the brain, its wealth of folds, its chemical composition—but without finding any sure connection to mental abilities. There are idiots with heavy brains and geniuses with light brains, and both can have the same shape of skull.

We know that the Chinese are able to learn other languages (such as English) quite easily. And with the languages come the ideas. Why should the Chinese be incapable of grasping them?

"Negroes have never created an Aristotle or a Plato," it is said. No, nor had the Greeks in the days of Ramses the Great. And in Aristotle's day, Northern Europeans had no Newton or Pasteur. That does not prove that the Greeks or the Northern Europeans were incapable of progress.

What a human being becomes does not depend only on the individual's personal qualities, but also on the society in which he or she lives and what tasks it poses. When the equals of Newton and Pasteur were born to the yellow or black races, they had not been given the materials with which to work or the problems to solve which led Newton and Pasteur along their brilliant paths.

The pessimists expect a new Dark Ages when the lower races take over the earth through "the foolish power of numbers." How is that to happen? If the colored peoples are really as inferior as is maintained, then we have nothing to fear from them. Then Europe will always rule the world.

But presume they are not so inferior, but are really able to threaten our position? Well, says Novicow, if they should turn out to be capable of catching up rapidly with us, why should they not also be capable of developing civilization further? Why then fear a new Dark Ages?

What will happen when the Asians seriously emerge into the market is the same as what has already happened a great many times. When Germany began industrializing, British industry was totally dominant. The Germans provided British firms with fierce competition as a result of their technical capacity and ability to organize.

Today, in a great many fields, German industry is as large as the British. And what happened to the British? Have they become poverty stricken? On the contrary, their prosperity had never risen more sharply than during the late nineteenth century.

If competition between the English and the Germans produced good results, then competition between the French and the Chinese will also do so—that does not depend on color of skin.

Presume, says Novicow, that Africa and Asia had as many railways and factories as Europe has today; presume that everyone there had had a higher education and geniuses were as common or uncommon as in Europe—would that really be a world to fear?

Of course, if thirty million Chinese soldiers invaded Europe and slaughtered everything that came in their way, that would be an enormous reverse for European civilization—not because those soldiers were yellow, but because they killed. It is far more likely that Aryans will continue to kill each other as they did during the Thirty Years War, than that we shall all be killed by the Chinese.

And if those thirty million come without arms, what will happen then? Well, if their methods are more efficient than ours, then we shall imitate them. If ours are better than theirs, then they will imitate us. Our civilization will be stronger, not weaker.

The population of the world is unevenly divided over the earth. Some parts are very highly populated, others sparsely so, which prevents any rational exploitation of the resources of the world. We should fight for a leveling of population, and the best way to do that is to remove the obstacles in the way of population flows that tend to create equilibrium.

To be happy on this earth, the whites must learn to overcome their racial prejudices just as they have begun to overcome their social prejudices. International democratization is just as necessary as a national democratization.

If we try to keep the Chinese away from the markets and work opportunities here, that will lead to hatred and determination in them. We will create the threat that we are aiming to avoid.

Novicow quotes Pearson, who considers that we are careless when we spread European technology to other parts of the world. "One day the Aryans will see with despair the way millions of yellow and black brothers are seizing their wealth and power," says Pearson.

It is an elementary mistake, Novicow objects, to think that one's gain is always another's loss. Progress is progress wherever it occurs. Pasteur was a Frenchman, but his discoveries have been to the benefit of the whole world. The day that Africa and Asia have reached further than Europe, we will also be able to profit from progress we ourselves have not been able to achieve.

And if the whites one day see with despair the way their yellow brothers are trying to seize power, with what despair then will our yellow brethren regard us, who already have the power? If our only aim is to hold them back, then their only aim will be to get rid of us.

"Ah, how miserable are the ideals of this relentless Englishman, who does not dream of any other future but unlimited exterminations and cruel bloodbaths. History is no joke, it is said. It certainly is not, if millions of people are to be massacred because they have a different colour of skin or shape of skull from ours," says Novicow.

Then he adds: "But history will at once become a trifle lighter the day we leave our childish and barbaric prejudices behind us and at last decide to respect the rights of all our equals."

18

"The dying negro"

Joseph Conrad, 1897

JOSEPH CONRAD'S THIRD novel is about a dying "nigger." He is dying on board a ship that symbolizes a whole society. At first the ship is close to being wrecked by a storm, then it lies paralyzed by calm weather. But as soon as the black man is buried, the wind rises and the ship again speeds on.

A variant of the myth of Iphigenia, of course. But why choose such a main character? Why that kind of action, or rather, lack of action?

Critics asked themselves that when *The Nigger of the Narcissus* was published in 1897. And despite the billions of words written since on Conrad's writing, that particular mystery still remains. I make no claim to have solved it. But I have a hypothesis.

If it had been an Indian lying there dying, there would have been no problem. As early as when Benjamin Franklin met the Paxton boys in 1764, "the dying Indian" was a common notion, and in the early nineteenth century he became a fashionable figure in literature. James Fenimore Cooper's successful novel *The Last of the Mohicans* (1826) released a "Last of" romanticism that cast an enchanted shimmer over the continuous extermination.

But the seaman dying in Conrad's book is black. And black people were not dying, but rather it was the other way round. They had been imported to replace the dying Indian—their ability to survive and increase their numbers in captivity was the actual reason they were in America.

Gradually, their ability to survive became a problem for white society. How could the "Negroes" be got rid of when there was no longer any need for them?

The first "solution" the whites hoped for was to be able to send the blacks back to Africa, or to some other place very far away. The idea had always been utterly unrealistic, says the American scholar Winthrop D. Jordan (1968), but all the same, it recurs with the founding fathers of the United States with all the stubbornness of an obssession. "Caught, as they thought, between the undeniable necessity of liberating their Negroes and the inevitability of disaster if they did, they clutched desperately at the hope that the problem would simply go away."

In the 1830s, the whites of the South began to talk about slavery in a new way—not as something shameful that would soon be abolished, but as a natural and permanent element in the social life of the South. Slavery, they said, was in the interests of the slave—freedom would be fatal to the black man.

This idea appeared at roughly the same time on both sides of the Atlantic. In 1839, one of the North's leading theologians, Horace Bushnell, maintained that if slavery were abolished, "vices which taint the blood and cut down life" would within half a century penetrate the whole stock and begin to "hurry them off, in a process of premature extinction: as we know to be the case with another barbarous people now fast yielding to the infection of death."

It was to the "dying Indian" he was referring. Only slavery protected the black man from becoming a "dying Negro."

That same year, a Scottish doctor, Robert Verity, published his detailed and theoretically very advanced explanation for the extinction of the dark races in *Changes Produced in the Nervous System by Civilization* (1839). It is a universal theory that anticipates both Gobineau and Darwin, but here I shall confine myself to relating the conclusions drawn on America's black people.

When the European races begin to be short of space in North America, says Verity, "the present numerous negro population will in all likelihood decline like the Indian races and in the course of time become extinct."

After their liberation from slavery "they will be unable to protect themselves against the competition of superior antagonists, and against the oppressions which a stronger race is but too apt to exercise upon a weaker."

We can "with the certainty of a law of nature" expect that contact between "the stronger and more intellectual races" and "the inferior and weaker" will lead to the latter going under. "Those which cannot assimilate will end by disappearing." As evidence, Verity refers to the high mortality rate of free black men in Philadelphia and New York.

A young doctor in Massachusetts, Edward Jarvis, considered he had found yet another piece of evidence for this thesis in the 1840 census, which for the first time accounted for the mentally ill and "idiots."

Jarvis found that among whites, the numbers of mentally sick in the North and the South were roughly the same. But among the blacks, differences were greater. In the South only one in 1,558 was mentally ill; in the North, on the other hand, the number was one in 162. Mental illness, in other words, was ten times as common among free blacks in the North than among black slaves in the South.

Jarvis drew the conclusion that slavery had a beneficial effect, while on the other hand freedom for the black man was an inappropriate state leading to illness and early death.

Many people leaped on to this bandwagon with gratitude. If freedom were damaging to the blacks, what then would happen if half a million blacks were suddenly let loose in Virginia? Where would mental hospitals be found for "tens of thousands of mad negroes"? Where were the prisons for thousands of black criminals? How could anyone live in a country in which one was confronted with criminals and the mentally ill on every street corner? No, slavery must be retained, both for the good of the black people themselves, and because their freedom constituted an unacceptable threat to the whites.

Meanwhile, Jarvis went on working with source material and found that many places in the North had registered all their blacks as "idiots" or "mentally ill." The information was clearly unreliable, and Jarvis apologized for having distributed it and allowing himself to be deceived into faulty conclusions.

The disclaimer naturally did not receive the same publicity as the first false but sensational statement—the myth that "freedom turns the negro mad" lived on.

During the 1850s, the tone sharpened in both those who were for, as well as those who were against slavery. "Pennsylvania has a negro population of 53,000," writes John Campbell in *Negro-Mania* (1851). "The plain fact of the matter is, that we must take efficient steps ere long to get rid of our negroes, either by colonization or otherwise; but get rid of them we must and must is the word."

George Fitzhugh in his *Sociology for the South* (1854) considered that the law of nature would solve the problem by itself. "It forces the stronger race to oppress and exterminate the weaker. The experience of the past shows that [the Negro's] present condition is hopeless; but make him property, and this same Anglo-Saxon will protect, guard and cherish him, for no people on earth love property more."

George Westen in *The Progress of Slavery in the United States* (1857) put greater emphasis on what was gradual and peaceful in the process, but held the same opinion of the final result. "The Negro will disappear . . ." The disappearance entailed no catastrophe, but was a beneficial result of the laws of nature. The only thing that hitherto had postponed the extinction of the black race was the artificial protection slavery provided.

A few years later, when the American Civil War was already in full swing, J. M. Sturtevant, President of Illinois University, explained that the abolition of slavery was the surest way of getting rid of the blacks.

In all populations there was a "lower stratum," he said in his *Destiny of the African*, that had insufficient income to support a family. This was the inevitable consequence of a law of nature which decided that only the strongest, noblest, and most vigorous specimens of the race should be allowed to reproduce themselves, while the weak, the evil, the decayed, and broken should be weeded out.

After the abolition of slavery, owing to competition with superior whites, the blacks sink to that lower stratum. The result is inevitable. "Negroes will never be able to marry, and if they attempt to build a family, their children will die in infancy, struggling in vain against the laws of nature. Like his brother the Indian of the forest, he must melt away and disappear for ever from the midst of us."

Well-meaning but ignorant philanthropists are about to eradicate the Negroes by attempting to educate them, said J. H. Van Evrie in *White Supremacy and Negro Subordination* (1868). To educate the blacks is impossible for simply physiological reasons, for if the black man is given a white man's head, which is what education entails, he is thus made incapable of standing upright.

At the same pace as the blacks are forced out of their normal state, slavery, into the white man's situation, freedom, at an equal pace, they will be approaching their annihilation. The white man's rights will become the black man's destruction. The free "negro" is destined to extinction.

All these pious hopes appeared to be put to shame when the 1880 census showed that the blacks in the South had increased more rapidly (forty-three percent in ten years) than the whites (twenty-nine percent). Edward E. Gilliam could already see a black deluge at his door. If the Negro population continued to increase at the same pace, in a hundred years it would amount to 192 million.

"This dark, swelling, muttering mass" will become increasingly restless and sullen under oppression until it finally takes revenge in outbursts of chaos and tumult. The only way to avoid catastrophe, according to Gilliam, would be to start immediately exporting the blacks. Just where to, he did not know.

But this time, too, a closer analysis of the figures produced another picture—the apparent rapid increase of numbers of blacks was due to previous under-reporting. Soon the "dying Negro" had regained his old place in the wishful dreams of the whites.

Dr. F. Tipton, a physician in Selma, Alabama, wrote in the *New York Medical Journal* in 1886, that neither the medical profession nor charity would be able to save the blacks from dying twice as rapidly as their white competitors. During the period of slavery, consumption had been practically unknown among the blacks but was now killing five times as many blacks as whites. Behind this "holocaust," as Dr Tipton called it, there is an as yet unknown factor. "The negro race will begin, at no distant day, to rival the Indian race in its rapid extinction in this quarter of the world."

One of the leading geologists of the South, Joseph Le Conte, in *Man and the State* (1892), guaranteed that the struggle for existence would in all certainty annihilate the weaker variants of humanity. "For the lower races everywhere (leaving out slavery), there is eventually but one of two alternatives, viz., either extermination or mixture. But if mixture makes a feeble race, then this is only a slower process of extermination."

The leading authority when it came to black mortality became the insurance statistician, Frederick L. Hoffman. His seemingly well-founded conclusions caused a sensation when they were first published in 1892. They were, to say the least, encouraging to those who wished to be rid of the blacks: "The time will come, if it has not already come, when the Negro like the Indian, will be a vanishing race."

Hoffman's book *Race Traits and Tendencies of the American Negro* (1896) was published by the American Economic Association, and for a long time was regarded as the standard work in the field. The high mortality rate among blacks was due primarily to innate deficiencies — "lower organisms and weak constitutions." An important contributory cause of death was "the comprehensive immorality that constituted a racial feature and which leads to scrofula, syphilis and even consumption."

The Negro had been in excellent health when slavery was abolished, but since then had degenerated without interruption. If this tendency continues, the number of deaths will soon exceed the number of births. "A combination of these traits and tendencies must in the end cause the extinction of the race."

When Joseph Conrad sat down to write *The Nigger of the Narcissus*, this was the last word of science on the question of the future of the blacks in America. The Negro was dying out. And once he was dead, the American South, freed from the burden of this inferior race, would at last again have winds in its sails and make new speed.

I do not maintain that Conrad's novel fights against racism in the same sense as do the other antiracists in this book. Conrad does not fight against anything—if not possibly lack of imagination and the inability to empathise with another person's situation. Conrad does not argue against racism, but rather he describes one of its most beloved dreams, which had apparently just received its final confirmation from science. He embodies this dream, and by subsituting abstractions such as "the dying Negro" and "the superior white man" with real people, he explodes it from within.

What happened then? How did things go?

The dream of "the dying Negro" still existed when William B. Smith wrote *The Color Line* (1905). "The doom that awaits the negro has been prepared in like measure for all the inferior races," he wrote. Even if it were possible to halt the downward spiral of disease and death, it would not be advisable, for there are diseases whose evolutionary function is to weed out the weak and preserve the future for the strong.

"All forms of humanitarianism that tend to give the organically inferior an equal chance with the superior in the propagation of the species are radically mistaken; to the individual and society they would sacrifice the race."

In his book *The Ultimate Solution of the American Negro Problem* (1913), Edward Eggleston discusses "on a strictly scientific footing" all suggested solutions, including deportation, sterilization, and physical extermination of all blacks. He finds all suggestions practically and politically unworkable and fundamentally also unnecessary, for blacks, as Hoffman had already predicted, were on their way to exterminating themselves.

Economic factors, slowly but surely, tend to reduce the number of blacks. Because of mental inferiority, the Negro finds it more and more difficult to earn his living when competing with the white labor force. A contributory factor is the black's often self-elected segregation. When blacks live entirely with blacks, their racial decline becomes more rapid and their mortality markedly increases.

Without close contact with the superior race, the blacks have a strong tendency to fall back into primitive living habits and a lack of personal hygiene. There is no reason for the whites to attempt to urge hygiene and morality in "negro quarters," as long as they can protect themselves from infection.

The Southern Negro will perhaps not disappear even for twenty generations, but within the course of a century the black population will be so reduced that it will no longer constitute a serious social problem in the United States.

Hoffman's and Egglestone's final solution of the American "Negro problem" was taken up for renewed examination by the Berkeley zoologist S.J. Holmes in his *The Negro's Struggle for Survival—A Study in Human Ecology* (1937). Holmes found that "the dying Negro" was no longer dying.

Before the first world war, European immigrants drove the blacks out of many occupations in the North. But when immigration was limited, blacks had their chance. The increase in the black population that occurred between 1920 and 1930 may be partly due to falling birth rates among white immigrants.

It is lower-class whites who compete for jobs with the blacks. Increased birth control and falling birth rates among the poor whites reduce the pressure on the blacks where this had been most noticeable. Reduced infant mortality is another additional reason for the expansion of the black race.

At the moment, it seems that both races are increasing the same pace at but, according to Holmes, the situation is unstable and it seems that the blacks will increase more quickly than the whites. Here, in 1937, a century after its first appearance in 1839, the dream of "the dying Negro" finally died.

What was there to hope for now? What could be done?

Presumably nothing will be done, Holmes says. The strange thing was that "peoples will fight to the death to maintain their rights against a hostile invader, but they will allow themselves to be outbred and supplanted by rival stocks without the slightest attempt to forestall their fate."

Was there no way out? Of course there was. It was called "population control".

"Should a marked increase in the relative proportion of blacks to whites become unmistakable, the whites may be led to consider seriously the problem of population control. Certainly one very useful function of government, could it be accomplished, would be the proper regulation of numbers in the interest of the general welfare," says Professor Holmes.

So if "the dying Negro" was no longer dying, then there were methods to help him along the way.

Nations often find it desirable to control their population's ethnic composition, but this entails a great many difficult and sensitive problems, Professor Holmes goes on to say. "The Turks went at the business in Armenia in a fashion that brought them little credit in the eyes of the civilised world." In Germany, there was much discussion about how to limit the number of Poles, Jews, and other elements disapproved of by the present [Nazi] regime.

Hitherto most attempts at population control have been governed by racial hatred, religious fanaticism, fear, or other less intellgent driving forces. This is unfortunately also the case in Germany, where many otherwise fine minds are seriously occupied with this problem.

If an American government should decide to regulate the proportions between blacks and whites, the professor considers, there are methods that do not really offend any fundamental human right.

"At present I am not venturing to give these gentlemen any specific advice; I am merely suggesting the possibility of humane and even feasible means of dealing with it."

The methods existed. The will existed, in a few. The wishful dream existed, in a great many. Even in the United States, and perhaps there in particular, the "final solution" had long been yearned for. But the counterforces were also strong, stronger in the United States than in many other countries. They were victorious. Professor Holmes never had the opportunity to practice his humanism.

19

"Equality or massacre"

Anatole Leroy-Beaulieu, 1897

On 27 February, 1897, Anatole Leroy-Beaulieu gave a lecture on anti-Semitism at the Catholic Institute in Paris. Right-wing extremists were there, and the anti-Semites sat in the front row, whistling and booing. Leroy-Beaulieu himself had invited them. He wanted to reach his opponents.

France was the first country in Europe in which the Jews gained citizen's rights. In the early 1800s, it was French troops who freed the Jews everywhere the French took power. France still regarded itself as the home on earth of equality and civil rights. But that picture was not entirely a true one.

Individual haters of Jews had, of course, always existed. Soon after the American Civil War, a French lecturer in Cairo, Eugène Gellion-Danglar, wrote a series of articles in which he maintained that the Jews, just like the Indians and blacks in the United States, belonged to a dying race.

It is a well-known fact, he says, that the inferior races everywhere are on the decline. That is so with the blacks, that is so with the Tartars, and that is also so with the Semites. A process of degeneration, which nothing appears to be able to halt, tips them over the precipice and will inevitably end with their total disappearance.

The Semite is a child doomed to eternal childhood. He also has all the weaknesses of a woman: he is cowardly, false, capricious, catlike, lecherous, and greedy. As an Oriental, the Semite is in general a frugivore (fruiteater), so weaker and less intelligent than a carnivore. The Hebrew also has a tendency to ichtyphagy (to eat fish), which leads to the fearful skin diseases common among the Jews of the Orient. All this shows that the Semitic race has now reached the limits of its abilities and is on the way "down the rapid slope leading to annihilation," says Gellion-Danglar.

In the 1860s, nonsense of this kind still had no real market in France. But times change. Defeat in the Franco-German War of 1870, the lengthy depression that followed, anti-Semitic agitation in Germany in 1879, the violence against the Jews in Russia in 1881, and the great bank crash in Paris in 1882, when hundreds of thousands of small savers lost their money—all these contributed to creating a climate in which Gellion-Danglar's wishful thinking could be taken seriously and be reprinted in *Les Sémites et le Sémitisme aux point de vue ethnographique, religieux et politique* (1882).

Gellion-Danglar died the same year as his book was published. His spiritual heir, Edouard Drumont managed to make anti-Semitism into a commercial success with his book *La France juive* (1886).

There was no originality in Drumont's ideas. He started out as his predecessor had from the fantasy of an "eternal conflict" between "the Aryan and the Semite," whose antagonism "has dominated the world in the past and will continue to trouble it even more in the future."

Aryans were of varying types, but one Jew, according to Drumont, was always like the next. All characteristics of Jews were innate; in fact Drumont even believed that "many Jews were born circumcised." The race was distinguished only by its negative characteristics: it had no mythology, no epics, no science, no philosophy, no literature, no art—and these deficiencies had their foundations in the biological inferiority of the Semite.

As the Jews by their race were hereditarily determined to do evil, they were beyond morality. They were not responsible for what they did. "They simply are like that," says Drumont. Like the Indians and the blacks, the Jews were compared with animals: vultures, apes, hyenas, jackals, foxes, pigs, rats, snakes, spiders, and lice, just to give a few examples. Such disparaging comparisons also provided an implied instruction on how they should be dealt with. Like rats, like lice.

This message was a roaring success in French homes in 1886. Drumont's book sold 100,000 copies in the first year, and the book was reissued in 200 editions during the author's lifetime. Had Drumont been a great public speaker with personal charisma, the masses could have carried him and his message to power. Fortunately, he was a timid, withdrawn journalist, utterly without qualities of leadership. But he used the income from his best-seller to found not only a newspaper, which daily agitated against the Jews, but also an anti-Semitic organization with local branches all over the country.

Naturally, Drumont did not bear all the responsibility for this landslide in French opinion. Several leading scholars of anti-Semitism (Poliakov, Wilson) warn of collective repression, of the unpleasant truth of how all-embracing racism was at this time. The antiracists, not the racists, were the minority.

Even the antiracists, without noticing it, were often steeped in the racist thinking of the day. Emile Zola's *J'accuse* courageously attacked anti-Semitism in the army, the church, and the judiciary—but his novels are strongly marked by biological determinism and contain portraits of Jews that are difficult to distinguish from those by the anti-Semites.

One of the very few who kept a cool head and had the courage to stand by his opinions was Anatole Leroy-Beaulieu (1842–1912), a Normandy nobleman, a liberal Catholic, and professor at the École des Sciences politiques in Paris.

Leroy-Beaulieu had spent many years in Russia, and in the third volume of his main work, *L'empire des tsars* (1881–89), he describes with great empathy the situation of the Russian Jews in overpopulated Jewish quarters in which several large families were crowded into the same room and managed to survive in this misery only thanks to their extreme cleanliness and their religion.

In *Les juifs et l'antisémitisme* (1893), he took up the struggle against French anti-Semitism. He tried to twist the nationalistic weapon out of the anti-Semites' hands and turn it against them. Anti-Semitism is a doctrine alien to French nature, he said. "It comes from foreign parts, from countries lacking our spirit and our traditions."

Those who captured Alsace-Lorraine from France in 1870 are now applying their racial theories to the French Jews there and calling them "Semites." The Germans have always loved to give their hatred a veneer of science. But "semitic" is a linguistic term that describes a language group—that there should be a corresponding biological race is only an assumption. To want to found the nation on a common race, as the Germans do, is just as backward as the Russians wanting to found theirs on a common faith. "All modern nations are racially mixed. We are all half-breeds."

So cultural fellowship is more important than biological. Let us quite simply admit, says Leroy-Beaulieu, that in disposition, abilities and intellectual habits, a French Jew, even if called a Semite, is far closer to us than an Indian Brahmin, even if he is called Aryan.

Perhaps this attempt to gain sympathy for French Jews against German anti-Semitism would have succeeded—if during the following year the Dreyfus affair had not given the anti-Semites the opportunity to point out a Jew as a German spy, and, consequently, all Jews as potential traitors.

It now became literally dangerous to take the side of the Jews. The extreme right recruited demobilized soldiers and young butchers into semi-military gangs who demonstrated on the streets of Paris. They were called "Friends of Morès" and sat booing in the front row that February evening in 1897, when Leroy-Beaulieu rose to his feet to give his lecture on anti-Semitism.

How was he to make himself heard? How could he get them to listen? What would you yourself have said?

"You anti-Semites offend my pride," he said. You ascribe to the Jew, as you call him, a significance that is no way whatsoever in proportion either to the number of Jews in France or to their position in our society. You enlarge the Jew in a way that offends my reason but even more my pride.

"It means nothing to me if other people humiliate themselves and declare themselves incapable of dealing with Jewish competition. But on my part, I have not that humility. My ancient French blood rises against the thought that I should declare myself inferior to the Jew. On the contrary,

I am convinced that both I and they manage excellently in competition. "To maintain our position in relation to other races, whichever they may be, I request nothing more than one single thing: equality before the law."

The booing changed to applause at this stage. Leroy-Beaulieu used the breathing space to point out the contradiction in the anti-Semitic message: How could the Jew be at the same time so powerful and so innately inferior? Was it not somewhat simplified ethnology to produce the "Aryan" as the only noble and elevated one, while the "Semite" was always and everywhere base and evil?

And if we agree with the anti-Semites that the Semite is an intellectually and morally inferior creature—what do we then do about Christianity? The blood that flowed in Christ's veins, the blood that according to the Christian faith has saved the world, that blood, gentlemen, was Semitic. The Virgin Mary, the Apostles, they were all Jews!

"Judas, too, don't forget that!" cried the anti-Semites.

That interjection was not difficult to parry. And the Catholic listeners had been given something to think about. Had Jesus belonged to an inferior race? Was His blood "sullied at source"? Many agreed with the lecturer when he asked them to "leave this pretentious and unscientific amateur ethnology to its fate."

The booing from the front row grew even louder when the lecture moved on to economic matters. Anti-Semitism, Leroy-Beaulieu said, was creating a new kind of socialism. "It is a naive socialism, an unconscious socialism, a socialism for those who do not understand where their ideas are leading them . . . a right wing socialism, if you so wish."

That was a far-sighted observation. But the anti-Semites believed that Leroy-Beaulieu never came to the point. They kept on shouting "Explain Rothschild's wealth!" and "You've said nothing about the Question!"

"I've said as much as you have allowed me to say," retorted Leroy-Beaulieu. "If you would allow me a few moments of silence, I will use them to give you the anti-Semitic standpoint."

Silence fell.

"So—presuming that the anti-Semites' description of reality was correct—what then do they have for a solution?" Leroy-Beaulieu said. "The solution most anti-Semites seem to prefer is special laws for the Jews."

"Hear, hear!" shouted the anti-Semites.

"They want a return to the draconian laws passed against the Jews in the late Middle Ages. I have studied those laws on the spot, in Russia, where they are still in force, and I can assure you that the anti-Semites are no more satisfied than they are here. On the contrary, those laws have given rise to even more hatred there than here, as can be seen from the recurring riots in south Russia.

"Special laws in the Middle Ages, if I may say so, were no exception. The whole of society was packed with privileges for some and exceptions for others. Equality before the law (*droit commun*) is a modern concept of French origin. Legislation dominated by that principle is simply incompatible with special laws from another century.

"And how is the Jew, the Semite, to be defined in legislation of that kind? Not as a religion, but as a race, you say. But how do you recognize a Semite? By his nose? Are we to legislate against crooked noses? In countries where black and colored people are deprived of their civil rights, race is established by color of skin. But the Semite is as white as we are.

Only his religion separates him.

"And when the Jews have themselves baptized to escape the special laws, you will have to supervise them so that they don't remain Jews in secret. You will have to create a religious police, to put it briefly, an Inquisition. We are back in the Dark Ages.

"The anti-Semites' second solution—emigration—is also medieval: banishment, exile. But remember that even Protestants and Jesuits were once banished from France. It is always the same old story. Violence against one group opens the floodgates for violence against other groups. You start with the Jews and end with the Jesuits.

"And to where are the Jews to be banished? Anti-Semitism is international. Anti-Semites in all countries want to drive the Jews out of every country. Who is to accept them? The problem appears to be insoluble.

"So, in practice," Lerou-Beaulieu summed up, "we are faced with the following alternatives: equality or massacre." He had seen the persecution of the Jews in Russia. He had involved himself against the genocide in Armenia, and now he saw with frightening clarity what was about to happen. And he lifted himself on the huge wings of French rhetoric to warn his compatriots yet once again:

"Either we must use against the Jews the methods that we branded as a relapse into Oriental barbarity when the Sultan used them against the Christians in Armenia—or we must grant the Jews the same rights as every other human being, without exception, without privileges, govern the country with laws that are the same for all, and measure all, whether Aryans or Semites, regardless of origin, with the same yardstick, the same justice, the same scales and the same weights."

Leroy-Beaulieu's courage and eloquence were not able to stop the wave of anti-Semitism. As anti-Semitism slowly weakened in Germany, it was rapidly advancing in the France of the Dreyfus affair. The year 1898 was marked by violent anti-Jewish race riots in fifty-five French towns. A few years later, the extreme right sent their shock troops, "hooligans of the King," to beat up an undesirable professor at the Sorbonne itself in order to stop him teaching. A lecture such as Leroy-Beaulieu's was no longer possible.

20

The Miss Marple of Anthropology

Mary Kingsley, 1897

"What makes the African continent so bad?" was the question asked in the English political weekly *The Spectator* on December 7, 1895, in an article under the heading "The Negro Future."

"It is in Africa that the lowest depth of evil barbarism is reached," the article went on. The African, it said, belonged to a race that had never founded an empire, never built a city, never developed any art. Since the beginning of time, the Africans have been stagnant, degenerate, and subhuman, "a people abnormally low, evil, cruel."

For the future, it could only be hoped that contact with a higher race, either in the form of the "ennobling influence" of the British Empire, or in the form of the Christian missions' "annealing quality" would perhaps be able to rescue the poor degraded black man.

"We know nothing of the Divine purpose," sighed the author of the article. "The destiny of the Negro may be forever useless in our eyes, as were the worms in those of Darwin's gardener."

This was, to put it briefly, the usual old article on the future of the Negro. The comment it aroused was much more unusual.

The great Charles Kingsley, the man who saw white chimpanzees in Ireland, had a niece called Mary, who had been to West Africa to collect small fish for the British Museum. To make his predictable reflections somewhat more piquant, the author of *The Spectator* article had linked them to this female explorer's recent return from Africa.

He should not have done that. For when Mary Kingsley herself wrote to *The Spectator*, it turned out that she had a quite different, very controversial and shocking picture of the African.

Mentally and morally, the black man is by no means an inferior being, she wrote, and he has a strong sense of honour and justice. "In rhetoric he excels and for good temper and patience, he compares favourably with any set of human beings."

She thought the barbaric rituals and customs attacked in *The Spectator* article were no stranger than the burial rites we usually admire in the Greeks of Antiquity. "Given a duly educated native of the Niger delta, I am sure he would grasp the true inwardness of his Alcestis far and away better than any living European can.

"I do not believe the African to be brutal or degraded or cruel. I know from wide experience . . . that he is . . . grateful and faithful and by no means the drunken idiot his so-called friends, the Protestant missionairies are anxious, as an excuse for their failure in dealing with him, to make him out."

The Spectator published "this shameless letter" with the comment that what she was really defending was torture, murder, and cannibalism.

Mary Kingsley realised that if she wished to make herself understood, she would have to express herself more fully and more clearly. The result was two remarkable books—*Travels in West Africa* (1897) and *West African Studies* (1899)—which provided a new and more realistic picture of the inhabitants of Africa, filled with respect, humour and self-irony.

The typical anthropologist of the 1890s was an armchair scholar in his study, piecing together the picture of Africa from explorers' reports. The archetype of explorer was the tough Stanley at the head of a gang of armed men and long lines of subdued black bearers. Explorers of this kind had always been in a hurry and the names of places in their reports often mean "I don't know" in the local language.

Mary Kingsley combined the scientist and the traveler, something that did not become common among anthropologists until the 1920s. She always traveled unarmed, mostly alone, and always with trade as an excuse. Trading is a common female role in West Africa, so as a business woman she was welcome and made natural contact with the Africans, both women and men.

Naturally this was not without its dangers.

> I am not afraid of any wild animal—until I see it—and then—well I will yield to nobody in terror . . . no one can manage their own terror. You can suppress alarm, excitement, fear, fright, and all those small-fry emotions, but the real terror is as dependent on the inner make of you as the colour of your eyes, or the shape of your nose.

Mary Kingsley had read about that in Joseph Conrad's *An Outpost of Progress* before she wrote it, and Conrad had in his turn read her before he wrote about terror in *Heart of Darkness*. We know that Conrad admired Mary Kingsley and she Conrad, but neither of them ever knew the impression they had made on each other.

Nor was either entirely free of the racial thinking of their day. But both questioned even the most established ideas on the colored races, that Africans, for instance, were some kind of large children. Mary Kingsley says: "These Africans have often a remarkable mental acuteness and a large share of common sense; there is nothing really child-like in their form of mind at all."

> I confess that the more I know of the West Coast Africans the more I like them. I own I think them fools of the first water for their power of believing in things; but I fancy I have analogous feelings towards even my fellow countrymen when they go and violently believe in something I cannot quite swallow.
>
> Although a Darwinian to the core, I doubt if evolution in a neat and tidy perpendicular line, with Fetish at the bottom and Christanity at the top, represents the true state of things. It seems to me—I have no authority to fortify my position with, so it is only me—that things are otherwise in this matter . . .

Spinoza for Mary Kingsley stood out as the high point of fetishism and the line of the poem "God of the granite and the rose, soul of the lily and the bee" depicts fairly faithfully one of the common concepts of the African West Coast. But she found nothing mysterious about her African friends. Most of them were neither dreamers nor poets, but quite ordinary farmers and traders.

Mary Kingsley was one of the first to realize that the "Negro" does not exist. "There is," she says, "as much difference in the manners of life between say, an Ingalwa and a Bubi of Fermando Po, as there is between a Londoner and a Laplander." African societies each have their own culture and their own identity; missionaries and administrators did great damage when they tried to break down these identities.

Trade is for her the only valid reason for a nation to meddle in the affairs of others, as trade is to the mutual benefit of both sides. Great Britain is in greater need of markets than other nations. And in West Africa there are excellent customers.

A climate "that eats up steel and hardware as a rabbit eats lettuce" is an excellent customer for a town that produces iron and steel. A country whose population "likes burying cotton goods in the ground and washing them by slapping them against stones, and even in many other ways actively assists the climate in these processes of destruction," is an invaluable customer for a textile town.

Trade for mutual benefit should be the lodestar of policies. But present British policies are not carried out by businessmen, but by gentlemen from Clubland, by amateurs who promote the interests of neither Great Britain nor Africa.

> We have killed down native races in Australasia and America, and it is no use slurring over the fact that we have profited by so doing. This argument however cannot be used in favour of killing down the African in tropical Africa. If you were tomorrow to kill every native there, what use would the country be to you? No one else but the native can work its resources; you cannot live in it and colonize it.

> This form of murder by a nation I see being done in the destruction of what is good in the laws and institutions of native races.

With this "murder by a nation," Mary Kingsley is very close to the concept of "genocide" as defined in 1944 by the Polish lawyer Raphael Lemkin, then taken up in the convention on genocide which—half a century after her book—was accepted by the General Assembly of the United Nations in 1948. She goes on: "In some parts of the world this murder gives you an advantage; in West Africa judged from any standpoint you choose to take, it gives you no advantage."

Great Britain's present bad policies in Africa cannot be changed without first eradicating an idea, namely the idea that the African is, as some say, "steeped in sin," or as others say, "a lower or degraded race." Those are essentially the same ideas in different guises; and as long as you continue to think these things, you will continue to act as you do.

To summarize her standpoint, it was not "the Negro future" there was reason to question, but the future of the British Empire.

But Mary Kingsley remained a daughter of the empire. As soon as her second book came out, she went to South Africa, where the Boer War was being fought, as a volunteer nurse to serve the same empire she had just attacked. She fell victim to an epidemic, and a few months later she was dead.

21

For a Democratic South Africa

Olive Schreiner, 1897

A SOLDIER CALLED Peter Halket has become separated from his platoon and is spending the night alone by his fire. All around him, the countryside is ravaged, the maize fields trampled flat, the villages burned down. The South African Company's troops are putting down the native "rebellion" in recently conquered Rhodesia. Halket is a mercenary and will be paid in land and "niggers." He will soon be immeasurably rich and his old mother will no longer need to be a cleaning woman back home in England.

But horrible memories penetrate his sweet dreams. In the dark all round him, he sees the decapitated head of an old Mashona man. His hands still move. He hears the women and children screaming with terror as he points his machine gun at them. It rattles like a reaping machine and the black heads lie in long rows like sheafs . . .

A wandering Jew sits down by his fire. That disperses those gloomy memories and Halket begins to brag to the stranger about his black lovers—they are better than white ones. You do not have to support them; and when you have wearied of them, all you have to do is to throw them out.

That is what it will also be like with the labor force. The company portions natives out to us, and we make them work whether they want to or not. "It's just as good as having slaves, you see, and then you don't have all the trouble of caring for them when they are old."

The stranger listened in silence. Then he starts asking questions.

"What gives England the right to give away not just a whole country, but a whole people, people of flesh and blood, and force them to work for you without pay?"

"They're rebels, aren't they?"

"What is a rebel?"

"The blacks are rebels because they fight against us."

"What about the Armenians, then? Are they rebels when they fight against the Turks?"

"No, what right have the damned Turks to conquer the Armenians' country?"

Well, that was just it. If the massacre of Armenians in Turkey was wrong, why then was the massacre of blacks in Africa right? If the Armenians were allowed to rebel, why had the Africans not the same right? In the end, to Peter Halket it is a matter of color: "We're whites and so are the Armenians, almost anyhow. And they're Christians, like us," he adds.

"Are you Christians?" says Christ; for naturally it is He who has made his way to the soldier's fire that night.

When the soldiers find Peter Halket the next morning, he is a changed man. He maintains that the "darkies" are men fighting for their country, just as we Englishmen would fight if the French came and wanted to take England from us. He maintains that it is just as wrong to shoot a black prisoner as it is to shoot a white one. So he is ordered to do just that—but frees the black man and is instead shot himself.

In short, he goes too far. It won't do to oppose those in command. What does one black more or less matter? "They have no feelings, the niggers; I don't think they care whether they live or die, not as we would, you see."

The story about Peter Halket exploded like a bomb in South Africa. The question of race in that country had always been a burning issue, as the Europeans liked the climate and stayed. The Dutch came as early as the seventeenth century, and slowly but surely began to push aside the African population. The San people, the so-called bushmen, resisted and were as good as exterminated by military campaigns during the eighteenth century. The Khoi people, whom the whites called Hottentots, died in epidemics, and the survivors became bonded servants and herdspeople to the whites.

When the English took over Cape Colony in the 1800s, the Khoi and San peoples had been reduced from about 200,000 to 20,000. There were also 25,000 black slaves there, imported from other parts of Africa. Twenty-two thousand Boers of Dutch origin were in power. Decade by decade, they extended their lands in constant battles with the native population.

In 1809, the British drew up what were called the Hottentot laws, which established that the Khoi and the San must be registered as workers on white farms, otherwise they could be arrested as vagrants and put to forced labor with a white farmer. Only the mission stations were exempt from the forced-labor laws, which increased antagonisms between farmers who wanted more labor and missionaries who wanted more pupils for their schools.

The leading missionary was the Scottish minister of the church, John Philip (1775–1851), whose name has always aroused heated and contradictory emotions in South Africa. He was sent there in 1819 by the London Missionary Society on a short administrative assignment; but when he realized the extent of the violation of human rights for blacks, he stayed for the rest of his life in South Africa and fought for their cause.

First of all, Philip demanded that the British Empire draw a clear boundary around the still independent native states and that their territories be respected. Secondly, he demanded that the abused Hottentot laws be abolished, as they constituted an obstacle to economic development. South Africa needed the blacks, not just as workers, but also as consumers, Philip maintained. As long as the labor force was unpaid, it lacked the buying power, which alone would enable the economy to flourish.

His argument made an impression in London, and the Hottentot laws were abolished in 1828. Competition for labor increased, the Boers were forced to pay for their laborers and on several occasions were actually taken to court for maltreatment of their workers. After ten years of this, the Boers had had enough. They left the British colony and went north—just as the North American settlers at the same time went west, the South Americans south and the Australians eastward.

The Great Trek and the founding of new Boer communities occurred at the expense of the previously independent native states. So the success of Philip's demands for human rights led to the hated forced-labor laws, already abolished in the Cape Colony, being moved and applied to other, hitherto independent native people.

The following wind of Philip's ideas of the 1830s changed to an increasingly fierce headwind in the 1840s. Racism was gaining ground all over the world. Philip lost his support in the British Parliament, and among the whites in South Africa he had always been a lone and hated man. He died defeated.

During his time of greatness, John Philip went to England to testify before a parliamentary committee. He recruited two new missionaries to return with him, the German Gottlob Schreiner and his English wife, Rebecca.

The couple spent fourteen years in the wilderness on various mission stations, where Gottlob showed himself to be in every respect a failure as a missionary—but a kind and playful father. Rebecca, on the other hand, was gifted, industrious, well read—but also harsh and punitive. She bore twelve children, of whom seven survived. They were brought up with an iron rod. One of them became prime minister of Cape Colony, another became South Africa's first major writer.

Olive Emilie Albertina Schreiner was born in 1855 and was named after her three dead brothers, Oliver, Emil and Albert. In her first novel, she writes about the solidarity between children that the violence of adults can create. "We will have the power some day . . . When I am strong, I'll hate everything that has power and help everything that is weak."

When she was twelve, her father was dismissed from his headmaster's post. She took her two younger siblings and went to live with their eldest brother, Theo. Between nineteen and twenty-six, she was a governess to various Boer families, lived a country-house life and wrote her first novels. Her first book, *The Story of an African Farm* (1883), also became her greatest success. At twenty-eight, she was an international celebrity, loved for her writing and loathed for her ideas.

For a missionary's daughter to be an atheist was perhaps not all that surprising. But she also became a militant feminist.

She protested against the Victorian image of women and the belief in their moral "purity." The sexual urge "is of equal intensity in both sexes," she wrote. "I don't for one moment believe in the moral superiority of women."

Just as little did she believe that women were biologically determined to weakness and helplessness—she had seen her mother run a household of fifty people. If nature is to be our master, then the female of most species is larger and stronger than the male, she wrote, and often even physically more active and dominant.

As a child, she watched the male ostrich daily relieve the hen at a fixed hour to sit on her eggs; and she watched too his tender care for the hatched young. She recognized her father and could not believe that the traditional roles of the sexes were determined by nature. The biological differences between men and women largely concerned the sexual organs and musculature, she wrote. Other differences were culturally determined.

There was, maintained Olive Schreiner, no scientific evidence that women were biologically inferior to men. Equally little evidence was there of blacks, Jews, Boers, or others that are called "inferior races" being biologically inferior men. That some groups, white men for instance, held a privileged position during a certain period of time did not mean they were born superior. Culturally conditioned inequality was only temporary and could not justify one race's permanent domination over another.

Obviously, Olive Schreiner was on a collision course with the anthropological science of the day, which reckoned it could place the races in a straight line of development from prehistory to the 1900s. Schreiner was (as was Mary Kingsley) one of the first to reject the straight-line anthropology and evaluation of races according to their supposed degree of "primitiveness."

The race question was to her all part of the labor question. In South Africa, the working class was black. In agriculture, mining, and industry, everywhere it was the blacks who did the work, the same work that in other countries was carried out by white workers for considerably higher wages. "Primitiveness"? It was nothing but a pseudoargument to keep wages low.

In John Philip's day, the British Empire had defended the equality of races. But that was long ago. Now territorial expansion and the hegemony of the white race had become the core of imperial ideology, as Olive Schreiner saw it.

For a brief while, she was captivated by Cecil Rhodes, his wealth, his power, his personal magnetism. But the massacres in Rhodesia opened her eyes. She broke with Rhodes and wrote the story of *Trooper Peter Halket of Mashonaland* (1897). Perhaps she was inspired by Dostoevsky's chapter on the "Grand Inquisitor" in the recently published *The Brothers Karamazov*?

The uproar was enormous, but the result disappointed her. She wrote: "In spite of its immense circulation [it had not] saved the life of one nigger, it had not the slightest effect in forcing on a parliamentary examination into the conduct of affairs in Rhodesia."

Olive Schreiner had promised herself she would "hate everything that has power and help everything that is weak." In the Boer War (1899–1902), it was natural for her to take a stand against the British Empire. After the war, she and her brother, Will, put all their strength into trying to create an independent, federalist, and democratic South Africa, based on equality between the races.

The greatest asset in the country was its racial and cultural diversity, she wrote. If the blacks did not receive the same economic and political opportunities as the whites, their suppressed talents would become "subterraneous and disruptive forces" and South Africa would be doomed. "If we raise the black man we shall rise with him, if we kick him under our feet, he will hold us fast by them."

No one listened. She was detested by the English for siding with the Boers, and by the Boers for siding with the blacks. She was detested by men because she was a feminist, and by South African feminists because she insisted on the vote for black women as well.

The South African Parliament drew up a constitution based on white supremacy, which was unanimously approved by the British parliament in 1910. The racial barrier became insurmountable. The statute prepared the ground for the Native Land Act in 1913, which allocated four million Africans to eight per cent of the land surface, while ninety-two percent was reserved for one and a half million whites.

Everything John Philip had fought for a hundred years earlier was now lost, and eighty more years were to go by before Olive Schreiner's dream could at last begin to be realized.

22

Denied Heritage

Theophilus Scholes, 1899

In the early 1880s, when Professor Edward Freeman was on a visit to the United States, a little bird whispered into his ear that "the best remedy for whatever was amiss would be if every Irishman should kill a negro and be hanged for it." This racist anecdote was fairly nasty even in the Europe of the late 1800s. William Babington reacted sharply, and Theophilus Scholes took it up at length as a starting point in his book *The British Empire and Alliances or Britain's Duty to her Colonies and Subject Races* (1899).

The title page says that Scholes had a medical qualification from Edinburgh. Nothing else is known about him. The name is Greek; and his pride in Europe's African heritage makes me think perhaps he was black, though that is no more than a guess.

"Freeman presents the spectacle of a man glorying in his own shame," says Scholes. He is an example of "the toxic use of history." The historian's task is not to exaggerate the exploits of his own race while looking down on other races with contempt and repugnance. Instead, Freeman should have asked himself—from where did Europe acquire the spark of civilization?

Well, where did it come from? The ancient Greeks believed it came from Egypt, the leading Mediterranean civilization during the millenium in which Greece was created. The Greeks wrote that they were colonized by the Egyptians and the Phoenicians, and that they received most of their culture from them.

When Europe began to take an interest in Hellas in the fifteenth century, it was not least because the Greeks were regarded as mediators of an even more ancient Egyptian wisdom. During the seventeenth and eighteenth centuries, European interest in Egypt was, if possible, even greater.

The change began with Napoleon's conquest of Egypt in 1798, and was completed a hundred years later, when Egyptian culture appeared to be nothing but a lengthy and sterile cul-de-sac. The Egyptians were thought of as white as long as they were admired; once they began to be despised, they were considered colored.

The romanticism of the early 1800s was born when Ancient Greece was made the core of European identity, says Martin Bernal in his learned and ingenious book *Black Athena—The Afro-Asiatic Roots of Classical Civilization* (1987), subtitled "The Fabrication of Ancient Greece." Romanticism idolized the Greeks, and as it was considered obvious that only racially "pure" civilizations could be creative, it followed that racial and cultural mixing in Ancient Greece had to be denied.

Linguists found the connection between Greek and Sanskrit and thus the Indo-European roots of Greek. They needed a historical explanation for this linguistic connection, and the idea of a conquest from the north fitted in. The Curtius brothers, the linguist Georg and historian Ernst, together concocted "the Aryan model."

"Impulse and motion are first communicated by Hellen and his sons; and with their arrival history begins," says Ernst Curtius in his *History of Greece* (1857). The greatest exploit of the Greeks was their language. "Greek must be regarded as a work of art . . . the whole language resembles the body of a trained athlete, in which every muscle, every sinew, is developed into full play, where there is no trace of timidity or of inert material, and all is power and life."

Curtius saw a direct connection between the Greek language and the Caucasian mountain landscape in which he thought it had developed before the Aryans invaded Greece. "One class of sounds is wont to predominate in the hills, another in the valleys, and again another on the plains," he says. It is inconceivable that such a beautiful and noble language as Greek could have arisen in the Mediterranean; even less so could it have been the consequence of the Hellenes mixing with Phoenicians and Egyptians.

It is true the Phoenicians had traded with Greece and the fact that they had invented the Greek alphabet could not be denied. But "racial science" had shown that the legends of Phoenician and Egyptian colonies in Greece were absurd:

> It is inconceivable that Canaanites proper, who everywhere shyly retreated at the advance of the Hellenes . . . and who as a nation were despised by the Hellenes to such a degree as to regard intermarriage . . . disgraceful, it is inconceivable, we repeat, that such Phoenicians ever founded principalities among a Hellenic population.

Many historians were still convinced that there were Phoenician colonies in Greece. "The real reason why people contest the existence of Phoenicians in Greece is that they object to make the Greeks indebted to Phoenicia for anything of importance," says Adolf Holm, who had not been overwhelmed by the wave of anti-Semitism of the 1880s.

In 1894, the Frenchman Victor Bérard still ventured to compare the Greeks with the Congolese and the Phoenicians with the Belgians and other Europeans who were just colonizing the Congo. "Why do we not see the similarities?" he says.

> When we talk about Asiatic influences on a European country, we cannot imagine . . . that barbarians could have ever dared come to us . . . An invasion from Semitic Asia of our Aryan Europe is repugnant to all our prejudices . . . This European chauvinism becomes a veritable fanaticism when it is . . . in Greece that we meet the stranger . . . We can only conceive of Greece as the country of heroes and gods. Under porticos of white marble . . .

The independent scholar Robert Brown, in 1898, still insisted on the evidence of Semitic influence on Greek culture. This was now considered an eccentric standpoint. The 1890s was the decade when Europe and North America achieved total control over the world. The indigenous people of America and Australia had been almost totally eradicated and the peoples of Africa and Asia had been conquered and humiliated. It seemed inconceivable that the conquered peoples had once been the teachers of their conquerors.

On the recently discovered "Minoan" frescoes were men

with black curly hair, but J. C. Stobart wrote in *The Glory That Was Greece* (1911): "I, for one, decline to believe that this fine fellow is a Semite or Phoenician, as has been suggested. We know that these people were extraordinarily gifted, especially in the sense of form, and that they were capable of very rapid development." So they could not be Semites, whatever they looked like!

By the time a new wave of anti-Semitism rolled across Europe in the 1920s, the Aryan model was already established. In the standard work *Cambridge Ancient History*, (1923) Professor Stanley Arthur Cook described the racial characteristics of the Semites. They possess little loyalty or morality, no perseverance, and are either too ascetic or too sensual. People of that kind could not have created Greek culture.

After World War II, overt racism became theoretically at least, unacceptable. But the Aryan model survived its racist premises. It has been questioned by scholars such as Micheal Astour and Cyrus Gordon, but their opinions are considered offensive. Europe still refuses to accept its Greek origins as a peripheral western example of another great civilization with its center in the Middle East and Egypt, says Martin Bernal.

That conclusion has naturally been highly controversial. It has been pointed out that Bernal ignores the fact that even when racist darkness was at its worst, there have always been antiracists criticizing and rejecting the Aryan model.

Theophilus Scholes was one of them. He maintained that the cradle of civilization lay in Africa. Greeks, Romans, Germanics, and Anglo-Saxons—they were all once primitive savages who had succeeded in elevating themselves thanks to their heritage from Africa. The black man laid the foundations of civilization and then went into retreat—perhaps to return one day and complete the building.

We must, says Scholes, free ourselves from the absurd misunderstanding that intellectual and moral capacity lies in our skins. The British Empire can be preserved and grow only if the attitude of the ruling race toward the subjugated races changes, so that the black people, who constitute the majority in many British possessions, also can see the empire as equally involved in everyone's interest.

The white races have succeeded in convincing themselves that God Almighty has created them as lords over not only animals and plants, but also over the rest of mankind. Two hundred years ago, this doctrine was accepted quite uncritically and the subjugated races believed in their own inferiority. But today there is a constantly increasing number among them who accept nothing else except equality between the races.

In the interests of the empire itself, their demands must be met, Scholes says. For we cannot expect that those treated by the British as "inherently inferior" are to show any greater enthusiasm for British rule.

Racial prejudice is a plague that appears to afflict the Anglo-Saxon race in particular. The sickness does not seem to reach the British Empire with the same violence as it does in the American South, but it is bad enough in India and South Africa. Fortunately, in England it is found in milder forms.

If we consider all the hatred and spite racial prejudices create, the oppression and persecutions they bring with them, the murders and mutilations, the way justice is corrupted and law and order undermined, the helpless grief and suffering of the oppressed, an empire divided into hostile camps instead of standing together with common interests—well, then we are forced to draw the conclusion that for the Anglo-Saxon race, racial prejudice is a worse disease than witch hunts and slavery once were, Scholes goes on.

Unless it can be proved that the Egyptians were white at the time when they were the most civilized people in the world, and the white races were black at the time when they were primitive tribes—unless that is proved, the theory that progress and greatness go together with whiteness, and inferiority with black skin, cannot be believed.

Racial prejudice rests on delusions, much as slavery and the burning of witches do. But like all other delusions, Theophilus Scholes ends, racial prejudices are also doomed to be exposed and dispatched to the grave of oblivion.

Sequence of Events

THE FOLLOWING IS a survey of events and publications mentioned in this book. The numbers in parentheses refer to the relevant chapter.

1733 English treaty with the Cherokees (14).
1752 English Crown breaks treaty (14).
1763 Cherokees retreat from large area (14).
1764 Franklin stops the Paxton boys (1).
1772 Granville Sharp wins the Somersett case (2).
1774 Long: *History of Jamaica* (4).
1775–78 Lavater: *Physiognomische Fragmente* (3).
1776–83 North American War of Independence (14).
1778 Lichtenberg: *Über Physiognomik* (3).
1784 Ramsay: *An Essay on the Treatment and Conversion of African Slaves in British Sugar Colonies* (4).
1787–1807 Abolition Society formed against the slave trade (4).
1789 Grégoire: Bill for the Jews (5) 13 states form the United States (10).

1791 Jews awarded citizen's rights in France (5); Cherokees lose more land (14).
1794 French slave trade banned for period (5); U.S. Cherokee Treaty (14).
1799 White: *An Account of the Regular Graduations in Man* (6).
1801 Cherokees refuse to give up more land (14).
1803 Winterbottom: *An Account of the Native Africans in the Neighborhood of Sierra Leone* (6).
1805 Cherokees forced to give up land (14).
1809 "The Hottentot laws" in South Africa (21).
1812 Napoleon frees Jews in Germany (13).
1815 Napoleonic Wars end. England superpower (8).
1816 Cherokees lose land (14).
1819 Anti-Jewish riots in Germany (13); John Philip to South Africa (21).
1822 Cherokee request to the Senate for protection (14).
1823–33 Anti-Slavery Society in England (7).
1826 Cooper: *The Last of the Mohicans* (18).
1826 Grégoire: *The Aristocracy of Skin* (5).
1828 "Hottentot laws" abolished (21).
1829 Rights of Cherokees invalidated (14).
1830 Bannister: *Humane Policy* (8); Indian Removal Act. Cherokees lose all territory and are moved (14).
1831 20,000 follow Grégoire to his grave (5); Tocqueville in United States (9).
1832 Lyell: *Principles of Geology*. Darwin in Patagonia (12).
1833 Slavery abolished in British colonies. American Anti-Slavery Society formed (7).
1834 Howison: *European Colonies* (8).
1835 Tocqueville to Ireland (16).
1837 Tiedemann: *Das Hirn des Negers* (7).

1838 Howitt: *Colonization and Christianity*, Bannister: *British Colonies*; Merivale: Colonization and Colonies. Aborigines Protection Society formed (8); Boers leave Cape Colony (21).
1839 Morton: *Crania Americana* (7), Verity: *Changes in the Nervous System Produced by Civilization* (18).
1839–42 First opium war (14).
1840 Tocqueville: *On Democracy in America, vol. 2* (9).
1841 Tocqueville in Africa (9).
1846 Senator Benton colonizes Asia (11).
1846–48 U.S.-Mexico War (10).
1847 Gallatin: *Peace with Mexico*. Simms: "Our destiny is conquest" (10).
1848 Revolution in Germany and France (7); Germany's Jews freed again (13).
1849 Gold rush in California. First anti-Chinese riot in United States (11).
1850 Anderson: *An Address on Anglo-Saxon Destiny* (10); Knox: *The Races of Man* (9)
1851 Campbell: *Negro-Mania* (18).
1852 Howitt: *The Literature and Romance of Northern Europe* (8); Beecher Stowe: *Uncle Tom's Cabin*; Ihering: *Geist des römischen Rechts* (14).
1853–55 Gobineau: *Essai sur l'inégalité des races humaines* (9).
1854 Nott & Gliddon: *Types of Mankind*; Fitzhugh: *Sociology for the South* (10, 18); Chinese lose legal rights in California (11).
1855 Squier: *Notes on Central America* (10).
1856 Parts of Gobineau's *Essai* in English translation (9).
1857 Westen: *The Progress of Slavery in the United States* (18); Curtius: "The Aryan model" (22).
1859 Darwin: *The Origin of Species* (10, 12).
1860 Pumpelly goes west (11).

1861–65 American Civil War. Black emancipation (15).
1862 Stout: *Chinese Immigration* (11).
1863 Marr: *Reise nach Centralamerika* (13); Sturtevant: *Destiny of the African* (18).
1865 Cherokees give up new land (14).
1868 Evrie: *White Supremacy and Negro Subordination* (18).
1869 Freeman: *Old English History for Children* (16).
1870 Pumpelly: *Across America and Asia* (11); Germany united. Jewish emancipation (13); United States again guarantees Cherokees land for all time (14); Franco-German War (19).
1871 Darwin: *The Descent of Man* (12, 14); First lynchings of Chinese in California (11).
1872 Amsa Walker's plan for the Indians (14); Stock Exchange boom in United States and Europe (11, 13).
1873-79 Financial crash and depression in United States and Europe (11, 13, 19).
1874 Ward: *Colonization in Its Bearings on the Extinction of the Aboriginal Races* (12).
1874 Green: *Short History of the English People* (16).
1875 High school in New Orleans segregated (15).
1876 Crop failure in California. Inquiry into "Chinese question" (11); Eliot: *Daniel Deronda* (13).
1877 Federal troops leave South (15).
1879 Eliot: *Impressions of Theophratus Such*; Marr: *Der Sieg des Judenthums über des Germanenthum* (13).
1880 Mommsen: *Auch ein Wort* (13); Hall: *A treatise of International Law* (14); Fiske: *American Political Ideas* (16).
1881–82 Pogroms in Russia. Mass exodus (19).
1881 Hunt: *A Century of Dishonor* (14); Dühring: *Die Judenfrage als Racen-, Sitten- und Culturfrage* (13).
1882 Chinese Exclusion Act. Race riots in California (11);

Freeman in United States (16, 22); Bank crash in Paris; Gellion-Danglar: *Les Sémites et le Sémitisme aux points de vue ethnographique, religieux et politique* (19).

1883 Schreiner: *The Story of an African Farm* (21).

1885 Berlin Conference divides up Africa (15).

1885 Cable: *The Silent South* (15).

1885–87 Anti-Chinese riots in California (11).

1886 Tipton: Black "holocaust" (18); Drumont: *La France juive* (19).

1887 Lagarde: "The Jewish vermin" (13).

1887–1934 Cherokee lands privatized and sold to whites (14).

1889 Hitler born.

1889–96 Roosevelt: *The Winning of the West* (16).

1890 The Massacre at Wounded Knee (1).

1892 Lynchings culminate: 231 victims (15); Le Conte: *Man and the State* (18).

1893 Pearson: *National Life and Character* (17); Leroy-Beauleu: *Les juifs et l'antisémitisme* (19).

1894 First massacre of Armenians. Girault: *Principes de colonisation et de législation coloniale* (14); Sino-Japanese War (17); Bérard: Criticism of European chauvinism (22).

1895 Babington: *Fallacies of Race Theories as Applied to National Characteristics* (16).

1896 Hoffman: *Race Traits and Tendencies of the American Negro* (18); New massacre in Armenia (19, 21).

1897 Robertson: *The Saxon and the Celt* (16); Novicow: *The Future of the White Race* (17); Conrad: *The Nigger of the Narcissus* (18); Kingsley: *Travels in West Africa* (20); Schreiner: *Trooper Peter Halket of Mashonaland* (21).

1898 United States takes over eight million blacks from Spain (10); Zola: *J'accuse* (19); Conrad: *Heart of Darkness* (20); Brown: *Semitic Influence in Hellenic Mythology* (22).

1899 Scholes: *The British Empire and Alliances or Britain's Duty to Her Colonies and Subject Races* (22).
1899–1902 Boer War (20, 21).
1900 Adams: *America's Economic Supremacy* (17).
1903 Nobel Prize to Mommsen (13).
1905 Japan defeats Russia (17); Smith: *The Color Line* (18).
1910 British Parliament approves white supremacy in South Africa (21).
1913 Eggleston: *The Ultimate Solution of the American Negro Problem* (18); Native Land Act reserves ninety-two percent of surface of South Africa for whites (21).
1921 Dühring: "Exterminate the parasitic races" (13).
1937 Holmes: *The Negro's Struggle for Survival* (18).
1944 "The Jew must be annihilated everywhere" (13).

Bibliography

1

Benjamin Franklin, *A Narrative of the Late Massacres in Lancaster County of a Number of Indian, Friends of this Province, by Persons Unknown, with some Observations on the Same* (1764). *The Writings of Benjamin Franklin*, Vol. IV (New York, 1906).

Ronald W. Clark, *Benjamin Franklin* (New York, 1983).

Winthrop D. Jordan, "The Discovery of Prejudice," in *White Over Black—American Attitudes Toward the Negro, 1550–1812* (New York, 1968; pbk. 1977). Hopkins and Woolman quoted after Jordan.

2

Granville Sharp, *Memoires*, 2 ed. (London, 1828).

David B. Davis, *The Problem of Slavery in the Age of Revolution 1770–1823* (Ithaca, 1975).

Susanne Everett, *History of Slavery* (London, 1993).

3

Johann Caspar Lavater, *Physiognomische Fragmente zur Beforderung der Menschenkenntis und der Menschenliebe* (Leipzig und Winterthur, 1775–78). First edition quoted after Gilman.

Georg Christoph Lichtenberg, *Über Physiognomik* (1778), reprinted in innumerable editions of Lichtenberg's collected works.

Cristoph Meiners, *Grundriss der Geschichte der Menschheit* (1793), quoted. Gilman.

Sander L. Gilman, *On Blackness Without Blacks* (Boston, 1982), chaps. 1 and 4.

4

James Ramsay, *An Essay on the Treatment and Conversion of African Slaves in the British Sugar Colonies* (London, 1784), chap. 4.

David Hume, "Of National Characters." in *Essays, Moral, Political and Literary* (1777) (Oxford, 1963).

Edward Long, *The History of Jamaica*, vol. II (London, 1774), book 3, chap. 1.

Frank M. Snowden, *Before Color Prejudice—The Ancient View of Blacks* (Cambridge, 1983).

Winthrop D. Jordan, *White Over Black—American Attitudes Toward the Negro, 1550–1812* (1968) (New York, 1977).

Richard H. Popkin, "The Philosophical Basis of 18th Century Racism," in Harold E. Pagliaro, *Racism in the 18th Century* (Cleveland, 1973).

Nancy Stepan, *The Idea of Race in Science—Great Britain 1800–1960* (London, 1982).

5

Henri Grégoire, *Essai sur la régénération physique, morale et politique des juifs* (1789), *Oeuvres IX* (Nenden, 1977); *Motion en faveur des juifs* (1789); *Oeuvres IX*; *De la littérature des nègres* (1808); *Oeuvres VII*; *De la noblesse de la peau ou du préjugé des blancs contre la couleur des africains et celle de leurs descendants noirs et sang-mêlés* (1826); *Oeuvres VIII*.

La Grande Encyclopédie, article "Grégoire."

Lord Ashbourne, *Grégoire and the French Revolution* (London, 1922).

Ruth Necheles, *The Abbé Grégoire* (Westport, 1971).

6

Thomas Winterbottom, *An Account of the Native Africans in the Neighbourhood of Sierra Leone*, (1803) (London, 1969), chap. 12, App. III.

Charles White, *An Account of the Regular Graduations in Man* (London, 1799).

Philip D. Curtin, *The Image of Africa—British Ideas and Action 1780–1850* (Wisconsin, 1964), chaps. 1–2, 8–9.

7

Friedrich Tiedemann, *Das Hirn des Negers mit dem des Europäers und Orang-outangs verglichen* (1837) (Marburg, 1984).

Samuel G. Morton, *Crania Americana, or Comparative View of the Skulls of Various Aboriginal Nations of North and South America, to which is Prefixed an Essay on the Varieties of the Human Species* (Philadelphia & London, 1839); *An Inquiry into the Distinctive Characteristics of the Aboriginal Race of America* (Philadelphia, 1844).

Stephen Jay Gould, *The Mismeasure of Man* (New York, 1981).

Robert E. Bieder, *Science Encounters the Indian 1820–1880* (Norman, 1986). Sanford B. Hunt quoted after Bieder.

8

William Howitt, *Colonization and Christianity— A Popular History of the Treatment of the Natives by the Europeans in All their Colonies* (London, 1838).

William and Mary Howitt, *The Literature and Romance of Northern Europe Constituting a Complete History of the Literature of Sweden, Denmark, Norway and Iceland* Vol. 1-2 (London, 1852).

Amice Lee, *Laurels and Rosemary—The Life of William and Mary Howitt* (London, 1955).

S. Bannister, *Humane Policy, or Justice to Aborigines of New Settlements* (1830; London, 1968).

John Howison, *European Colonies in Various Parts of the World Viewed in Their Social, Moral and Physical Condition* (London, 1834).

D. Coates a/o: *Evidence on Aborigines* (London, 1837).

Herman Merivale, *Colonization and Colonies* (London, 1861).

9

Alexis de Tocqueville, *De la démocratie en Amérique (1835–40). Oeuvres complètes*, I (Paris, 1951; *Oeuvres complètes*, III:2, V:2, IX (Paris, 1957–62).

Anders Ehnmark, *Slottet* (*The Palace*) (Stockholm, 1990).

André Jardin, *Tocqueville—A Biography* (London, 1988).

Robert Knox, *The Races of Man—A Fragment* (London, 1850) Lecture 6.

Arthur de Gobineau, *Essai sur l'inégalité des races humaines* (1853–55), *Oeuvres*, I (Paris, 1983). First presented in English as *The Moral and Intellectual Diversity of Races*, Philadelphia 1856.

E. J. Young, *Gobineau und der Rassisimus—Eine Kritik der anthropologischen Geschichtstheorie*, vol.4, *Archiv für Vergleichende Kulturwissenschaft*, (Meisenheim, 1968).

Michael Biddis, *Father of Racist Ideology—The Social and Political Thought of Count Gobineau* (London, 1970).

10

Charles Anderson, *An Address on Anglo-Saxon Destiny* (Cincinnati, 1850).

Reginald Horsman, *Race and Manifest Destiny—The Origins of American Racial Anglo-Saxonism* (Harvard, 1981). Simms, Thompson, Brown, Pollock and Merchants Magazine, quoted after Horsman.

Edward M. Burns, *The American Idea of Mission—Concepts of National Purpose and Destiny* (New Brunswick, 1957).

Robert E. Bieder, *Science Encounters the Indian 1820–1880* (Norman, 1986).

J. C. Nott & George R. Giddon, *Types of Mankind or Ethnological Researches*, 6th Ed (Philadelphia, 1854).

E. G. Squier, *Notes on Central America* (New York, 1855), chap. 3.

11

Raphael Pumpelly, *Across America and Asia—Notes of a Five Years Journey Around the World and of Residence in Arizona, Japan and China* 3rd ed. (London, 1870).

Friedrich Ratzel, *Die chinesische Auswanderung* (Breslau, 1876).

George F. Seward, *Chinese Immigration in its Social and Economical Aspects* (New York, 1881).

Johan L. Lalor, *Cyclopaedia of Political Science* (Chicago, 1881–1888).

Thomas F. Gossett, *Race—The History of an Idea in America* (New, York 1965). Benton quoted after Gossett.

Stuart C. Miller, *The Unwelcome Immigrant—The American Image of the Chinese 1785–1882* (Berkeley, 1969). Stout's report quoted after Miller.

Jack Chen, *The Chinese in America* (San Francisco, 1980).

12

J. Langfield Ward, *Colonization in its Bearing on the Extinction of the Aboriginal Races* (Leek, 1874).

Charles Darwin, *The Voyage of the Beagle* (1839) London, 1906.

Charles Darwin, *The Descent of Man* (1871), Princeton, 1981. chaps. 5 and 6.

Adrian Desmond & James Moore, *Darwin* (London, 1991).

Sven Lindqvist, *Exterminate All the Brutes* (Stockholm, 1992; New Press, 1996).

13

Raphael & Jennifer Patai, *The Myth of the Jewish Race* (1975) (Detroit, 1989).

Eugen Duhring, *Die Judenfrage als Racen- , Sitten- und Culturfrage*, 2d ed. (Karlsruhe und Leipzig, 1881).

George M. Fredrickson, *The Black Image in the White Mind—The Debate on Afro-American Character and Destiny 1817–1914* (New York, 1971).

Wilhelm Marr, *Reise nach Central-Amerika* (1863) (Hamburg, 1870). *Der Sieg des Judenthums über das Germanenthum—Von nicht confessionellen Standpunkt aus betrachtet* (12 Aufl. Bern, 1879).

Moshe Zimmermann, *Wilhelm Marr, The Patriarch of Anti-Semitism* (Oxford, 1986).

George Eliot, *Daniel Deronda* (London, 1876). *Impressions of Theophrastus Such* (London, 1879).

Walter Boehlich, (ed.), *Der Berliner Antisemitismusstreit* (Frankfurt am Main, 1965). Annotated anthology with all the important contributions to the debate.

Richard S. Levy, *Anti-Semitism in the Modern World* (Lexington, 1991). Annotated anthology, extracts from Treitischke and Marr in English.

Theodor Mommsen, *Auch ein Wort über unser Judenthum* (1880), quoted after Boehlich.

Michael A. Meyer, "Great Debate on Antisemitism—Jewish Reaction to New Hostility in Germany 1879–1881," *Yearbook of the Leo Baeck Institute* 11 (1966).

Alexander Bein, "Der Judische Parasit," *Vierteljahrshefte für Zeitgesichte* (1965), 121ff; *Die Judenfrage—Biographie eienes Weltproblems* (Stuttgart, 1980), chaps. 1–2.

Paul de Lagarde: "Juden und Indogermanen" (1887) reprinted in: *Scheiften für das deutsche Volk* (München, 1934).

14

Helen Hunt Jackson, *A Century of Dishonor—A Sketch of the U.S. Government's Dealings With Some of the Indian Tribes* (Boston, 1881).

William Edward Hall, *A Treatise on International Law* (1880) (Oxford, 1924). chap. 2.

Arthur Girault, *Principes de colonisation et de Législation coloniale* (1894) Paris 1907. chap. I:7. Thering quoted after Girault.

Ruth Odell, *Helen Hunt Jackson* (Univ. of Nebraska Press, 1937).

Ronald T. Takaki, *Iron Cages—Race and Culture in 19th Century America* (London, 1979). Walker quoted after Takaki, ch. 8.

Brian W. Dippie, *The Vanishing American—White Attitudes and U.S. Indian Policy* (Middletown, 1982).

15

George W. Cable, *The Silent South* (1885; New York, 1899).

Arlin Turner, *George W. Cable, A Biography* (Durham, 1956).

C. Vann Woodward, *The Strange Career of Jim Crow* (New, York 1966).

16

Charles Kingsley, *Letters and Memories*, vol. I (London, 1877). July 4, 1860.

William D. Babington, *Fallacies of Race Theories as Applied to National Characteristics* (London, 1895).

John Mackinnon Robertson, *The Saxon and the Celt—A Study in Sociology* (London, 1897).

Edward Freeman, *Old English History for Children* (1869); (London 1901); *Lectures to American Audiences* (London, 1882); *Some Impressions of the United States* (London, 1883).

John R. Green, *Short History of the English People* (London, 1874).

John Fiske, *American Political Ideas Viewed from the Standpoint of Universal History—Three Lectures Delivered at the Royal Institution of Great Britain in May 1880* (New York, 1885).

Theodore Roosevelt, *The Winning of the West* (1889–96) (New York, 1926), chap. 1.

17

Jacques Novicow, *L'Avenir de la race blanche—Critique du pessimisme contemporain* (Paris, 1897); *L'affranchissement de la Femme* (Paris, 1903). *La critique du darwinisme social* (Paris, 1910).

Brooks Adams, *America's Economic Supremacy* (New York, 1900).

Charles Pearson, *National Life and Character* (London, 1983).

Heinz Gollwitzer, *Die Gelbe Gefahr, Geschichte eines Schlagwortes, Studien zum imperialistischen Denken* (Gottingen, 1962).

18

Joseph Conrad, *The Nigger of the Narcissus* (1897) (New York, 1979).

Winthrop D. Jordan, *White Over Black—American Attitudes toward the Negro, 1550–1812.* (1968) (New York, 1977), chap. 5.

Sander L. Gilman, *On Blackness Without Blacks—Essays on the Image of the Black in Germany* (Boston 1982), chap. 1.

Bushnell, Westen, Sturtevant, Gilliam, Le Conte, and Smith quoted after George M. Fredrickson, *The Black Image in the White Mind—The Debate on Afro-American Character and Destiny, 1817–1914* (New, York 1971), chaps. 5, 8, 9.

Robert Verity, *Changes Produced in the Nervous System by Civilization, Considered According to the Evidence of Physiology and the Philosophy of History*, 2d ed., enlarged (London & Paris, 1839).

Jarvis and Tipton quoted after Willian Stanton, *The Leopard's Spots—Scientific Attitudes Towards Race in America, 1815–1859* (Chicago, 1960).

John Campbell, *Negro-Mania, Being an Examination of the Falsely Assumed Equality of the Various Races of Men* (Philadelphia, 1851), chaps. 6, 15, 23.

George Fitzhugh, *Sociology for the South or the Failure of Free Society* (Richmond, 1854).

Frederick L. Hoffman, *Race Traits and Tendencies of the American Negro* (Washington, 1896).

Edward Eggleston, *The Ultimate Solution of the American Negro Problem* (Boston, 1913).

S. J. Holmes, *The Negro's Struggle for Survival—A Study in Human Ecology* (Berkeley, 1937).

19

Anatole Leroy-Beaulieu, *L'Empire des tsars*, vol. 3, pp.613–42 (Paris, 1889); *Les Juifs et l'antisémitisme—Israel chez les nations* (Paris, 1893); "Les Armeniens et la question armenienne," conférence, 9 June 1896, Paris; "L'Antisémitisme," conférence 27 February 1897, Paris.

René Stourm, "Notice sur . . . Anatole Leroy-Beaulieu", *Institut de France* (Paris, 1914), vol. 22, pp. 95–120.

Eugène Gellion-Danglar, *Les Sémites et le Sémitisme aux points de vue ethographique, religieux et politique* (Paris, 1882).

Edouard Drumont, *La France juive* (Paris, 1886).

Stephen Wilson, *Ideology and Experience—Antisemitism in France at the Time of the Dreyfus Affair* (London & Toronto, 1980).

Albert S. Lindemann, *The Jew Accused—Three Anti-Semitic Affairs, Dreyfus, Beilis, Frank, 1894–1915* (Cambridge, 1991).

Leon Poliakov, "Histoire de l'antisémitisme," vol. 3, *L'Europe suicidaire 1870–1933* (Paris, 1977).

Robert Wistrich, *Anti-Semitism—The Longest Hatred* (London, 1991).

20

Mary Kingsley, *Travels in West Africa* (London, 1897); *West African Studies* (London, 1899).

Paul B. Rich, *Race and Empire in British Politics* (Cambridge, 1986).

Katherine Frank, *A Voyager Out—The Life of Mary Kingsley* (London, 1987).

Raphael Lemkin, *Axis Rule in Occupied Europe* (Washington, 1944).

21

Olive Schreiner, *The Story of an African Farm* (London, 1883); *Trooper Peter Halket of Mashonaland* (London, 1897).

Ruth First & Ann Scott, *Olive Schreiner* (London, 1980).

Joyce A. Berkman, *The Healing Imagination of Olive Schreiner—Beyond South African Colonialism* (Amherst, 1989).

John Philip, *Researches in South Africa Illustrating the Civil, Moral and Religious Condition of the Native Tribes* (London, 1828).

Thomas Pringle, *Narrative of a Residence in South Africa* (1835); (Cape Town, 1966).

W. M. Macmillan, *The Cape Colour Question—A Historial Survey* (Cape Town, 1968).

Andrew Ross, *John Philip, Missions, Race and Politics in South Africa* (Aberdeen, 1986).

Neil Parsons, *A New History of South Africa* (London, 1993).

22

Theophilus Scholes, *The British Empire and Alliances or Britain's Duty to Her Colonies and Subject Races* (London, 1899).

Martin Bernal, *Black Athena—The Afro-Asiatic Roots of Classical Civilization*, vol. 1; *The fabrication of Ancient Greece* (London, 1987).

Ernest Curtius, *Griechische Geschichte, Erstes Buch*, vol. I-II (Berlin, 1857).

Adolf Holm, *Geschichte Griechenlands*, vol. I (Berlin, 1886).

Victor Bérard, *De l'origin des cultes arcadiens* (Paris, 1894). *Bibliothèques des écoles françaises d'Athènes et de Rome*, 67.

John C. Stobart, *The Glory That Was Greece* (Philadelphia, 1911).

Robert Brown, *Semitic Influence in Hellenic Mythology* (London, 1898). Cambridge Ancient History, vol. 1, chaps. 5: 2 "The Semites. Temperament and Thought" (Cambridge, 1923).